LIFE
LIGHT
MAMMAL
MANET
MATTER
MEDIA & COMMUNICATIONS

MONET
MONEY
MUMMY
MUSIC
MYTHOLOGY
NORTH AMERICAN INDIAN
OCEAN
OLYMPICS

PERSPECTIVE
PIRATE
PLANT
POND & RIVER
PREHISTORIC LIFE
PRESIDENTS
PYRAMID
RELIGION

RENAISSANCE
REPTILE
RESCUE
SEASHORE
SHAKESPEARE

SHARK
SHELL
SHIPWRECK
SPORTS
SPY

SUBMARINE
SUPER BOWL
TECHNOLOGY
TRAIN
TREE

UNIVERSE
VAN GOGH
VIKING
WHALE
WILD WEST

WITCHES & MAGIC-MAKERS
WORLD WAR I
WORLD WAR II

11/04

Eyewitness
PLANT

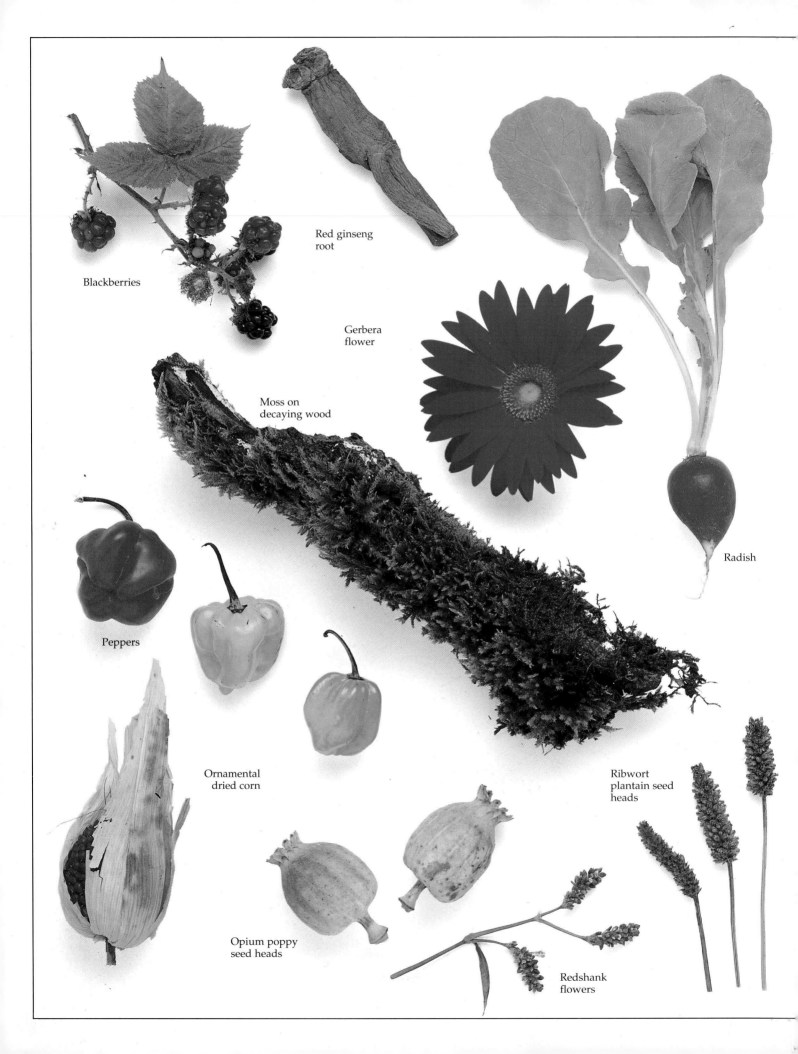

Blackberries

Red ginseng
root

Gerbera
flower

Moss on
decaying wood

Radish

Peppers

Ornamental
dried corn

Opium poppy
seed heads

Ribwort
plantain seed
heads

Redshank
flowers

Delphinium
flowers

Eyewitness
PLANT

Garden
pansies

Written by
DAVID BURNIE

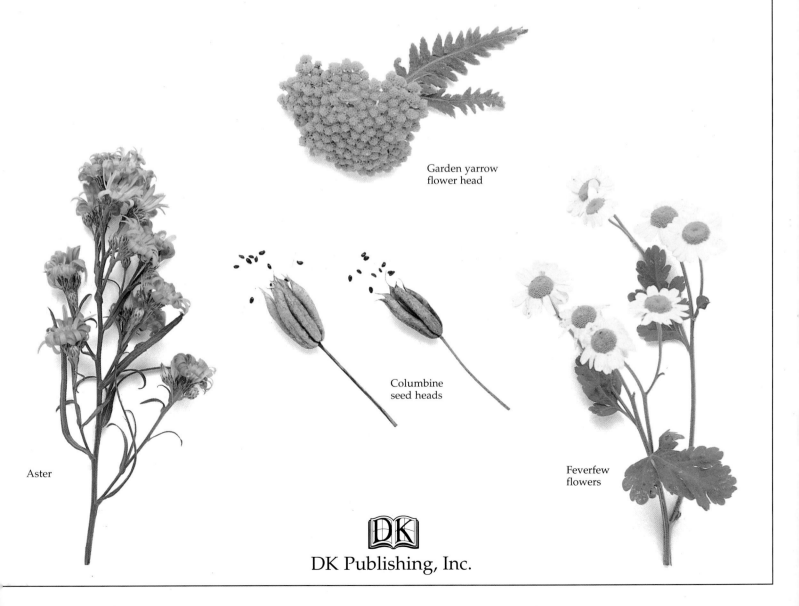

Garden yarrow
flower head

Columbine
seed heads

Aster

Feverfew
flowers

DK

DK Publishing, Inc.

Ripe fig cut
in half

Poppy
seed
head

Eucalyptus
leaves

Field
scabious

Common sorrel

Creeping
crowfoot

DK

LONDON, NEW YORK, MELBOURNE,
MUNICH, and DELHI

Project editor Helen Parker
Senior editor Sophie Mitchell
Senior art editor Julia Harris
Managing editor Sue Unstead
Managing art editor Roger Priddy
Special photography
Andrew McRobb of the Royal Botanic Gardens, Kew
Karl Shone, Kim Taylor, and Jane Burton
Editorial consultants
The staff of the Natural History Museum, London
and the Royal Botanic Gardens, Kew

PAPERBACK EDITION
Managing editor Andrew Macintyre
Managing art editor Jane Thomas
Editor Karen O'Brien
Art editor Ann Cannings
Production Jenny Jacoby
Picture research Lorna Ainger
DTP designer Siu Yin Ho

U.S. editor Elizabeth Hester
Senior editor Beth Sutinis
Art director Dirk Kaufman
U.S. production Chris Avgherinos
U.S. DTP designer Milos Orlovic

This Eyewitness ® Guide has been conceived by
Dorling Kindersley Limited and Editions Gallimard

This edition published in the United States in 2004
by DK Publishing, Inc., 375 Hudson Street, New York, NY 10014

04 05 06 07 08 10 9 8 7 6 5 4 3 2 1

A catalog record for this book is available from the Library of Congress.

ISBN 0-7566-0715-9 (HC) 0-7566-0714-0 (Library Binding)

Color reproduction by Colourscan, Singapore
Printed in China by Toppan Printing Co. (Shenzhen), Ltd.

Discover more at
www.dk.com

Yarrow
leaf

Cow
vetch

Common
toadflax

Oxeye
daisy

Cuckoo-
pint

Flower
of blue
echeveria

Bull
thistle

Contents

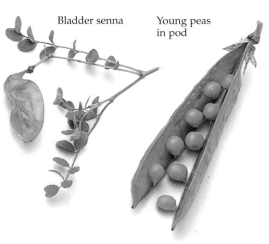

Bladder senna   Young peas
in pod

6
What is a plant?

8
The parts of a plant

10
A plant is born

12
Bursting into bloom

14
A light diet

16
A simple flower dissected

18
A complex flower

20
All sorts of flowers

22
How a plant is pollinated

24
Strange pollinators

26
From flower to fruit

28
How seeds are spread

30
Borne on the wind

32
Spreading without seeds

34
Living leaves

36
Self-defense

38
Creepers and climbers

40
Meat eaters

42
Caught in a trap

44
Parasitic plants

46
Plant passengers

48
Adapting to water

50
Surviving above the snowline

52
Living without water

54
Food from plants

56
The story of wheat

58
Potions and poisons

60
The plant collectors

62
Looking at plants

64
Did you know?

66
Plant classification

68
Find out more

70
Glossary

72
Index

What is a plant?

PLANTS ARE THE KEY to life on Earth. Without them many other living organisms would soon disappear. This is because higher life forms depend on plants, either directly or indirectly, for their food. Most plants, however, are able to make their own food using sunlight. All plants fall into two basic categories. Flowering plants, which this book looks at in some detail, produce true flowers. The nonflowering plants include "primitive" plants, such as mosses, ferns, horsetails, and liverworts, and the gymnosperms, a group of plants which includes the conifers, like the giant sequoias, shown opposite. There are about a quarter of a million species of flowering plants in the world today, and they grow almost everywhere from snowy mountain slopes to arid deserts. This book tells their story.

Lichen

THIS IS NOT A PLANT
It is often difficult to tell simple plants and animals apart. This plantlike organism is a hydrozoan and lives in the sea. Its "branches" are formed by tiny animals called polyps, which have tentacles to trap particles of food.

THIS IS A PLANT
A lichen is made up of two different organisms: a tiny nonflowering plant called an alga, and a fungus. The algal cells live among the tiny threads formed by the fungus and supply the fungus with food, which they make using sunlight (pp. 14-15). The fungus cannot make its own food and would die without the alga. Lichens grow very slowly and are extremely long-lived.

Lichens growing on limestone rock

THIS WAS A PLANT
Forests of horsetails and giant club-mosses, up to 150 ft (45 m) tall, once formed a large part of the Earth's vegetation (right). Over 300 million years, their remains have turned into coal.

Horsetail

MODERN RELATIONS
Ferns and horsetails are primitive plants that do not have flowers but reproduce by spores. Both first appeared nearly 300 million years ago. Although there are still many types of fern, only 30 species of horsetail live on Earth today.

Spores

Hart's-tongue fern

6

THE BIGGEST AND THE SMALLEST
The world's most massive plants are conifers – the giant sequoias of California, which can reach heights of over 310 ft (95 m). The smallest flowering plant is the rootless duckweed which is 0.01 in (0.3 mm) across.

Ribbon-like "thallus" divides into branches as it grows

Garden pansy

LIVERWORTS
Liverworts are nonflowering plants that live in damp places and reproduce by means of spores.

MOSSES
Mosses do not have flowers. Like liverworts, they reproduce by means of tiny spores.

LIVING SCULPTURES
Algae are simple, nonflowering plants. A diatom is a single-celled alga which has a rigid transparent case, or frustule, made of silica, a glasslike substance. This microscope photograph shows many species of diatom, each of which has a frustule of a different shape and pattern.

FLOWERING PLANTS
Unlike the other plants on these two pages, these have true flowers. They are also unique in having seeds which develop inside a protective structure called an ovary (p. 17). This later develops into a fruit (pp. 26-27). The garden pansy is a typical flowering plant.

GREEN BLANKETS
Some species of aquatic algae form long chains of cells, creating slimy blanket-weed.

Spirogyra blanket-weed

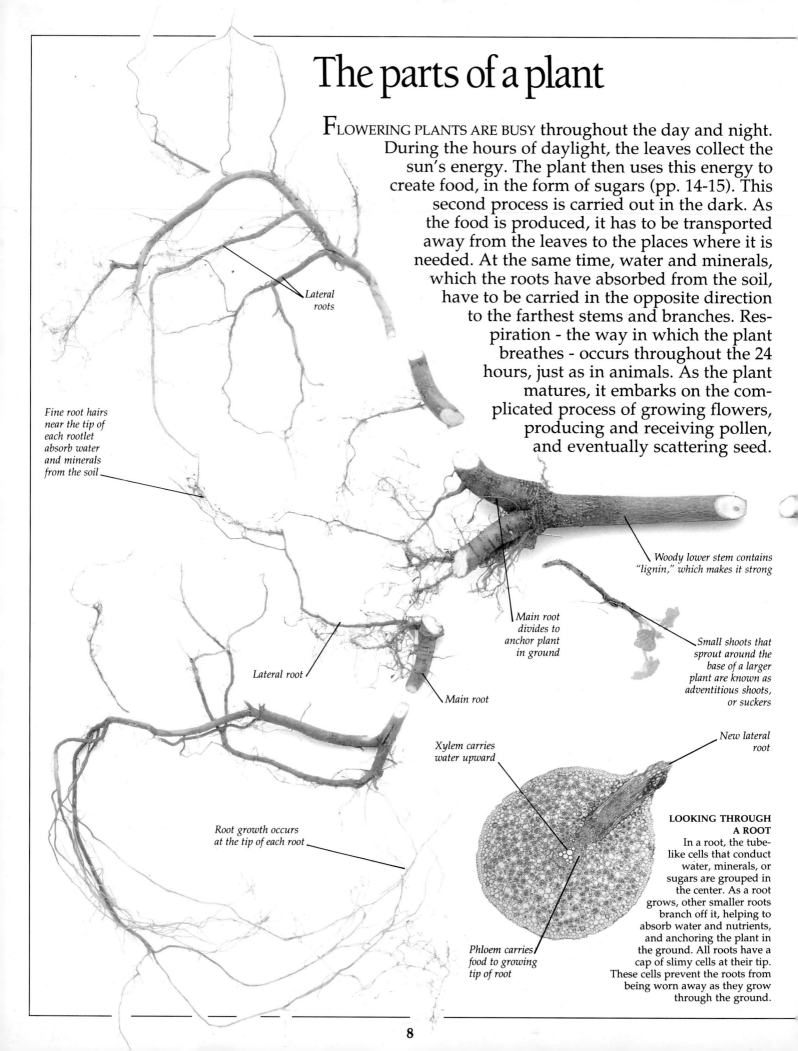

The parts of a plant

FLOWERING PLANTS ARE BUSY throughout the day and night. During the hours of daylight, the leaves collect the sun's energy. The plant then uses this energy to create food, in the form of sugars (pp. 14-15). This second process is carried out in the dark. As the food is produced, it has to be transported away from the leaves to the places where it is needed. At the same time, water and minerals, which the roots have absorbed from the soil, have to be carried in the opposite direction to the farthest stems and branches. Respiration - the way in which the plant breathes - occurs throughout the 24 hours, just as in animals. As the plant matures, it embarks on the complicated process of growing flowers, producing and receiving pollen, and eventually scattering seed.

Lateral roots

Fine root hairs near the tip of each rootlet absorb water and minerals from the soil

Woody lower stem contains "lignin," which makes it strong

Main root divides to anchor plant in ground

Small shoots that sprout around the base of a larger plant are known as adventitious shoots, or suckers

Lateral root

Main root

New lateral root

Xylem carries water upward

Root growth occurs at the tip of each root

LOOKING THROUGH A ROOT
In a root, the tube-like cells that conduct water, minerals, or sugars are grouped in the center. As a root grows, other smaller roots branch off it, helping to absorb water and nutrients, and anchoring the plant in the ground. All roots have a cap of slimy cells at their tip. These cells prevent the roots from being worn away as they grow through the ground.

Phloem carries food to growing tip of root

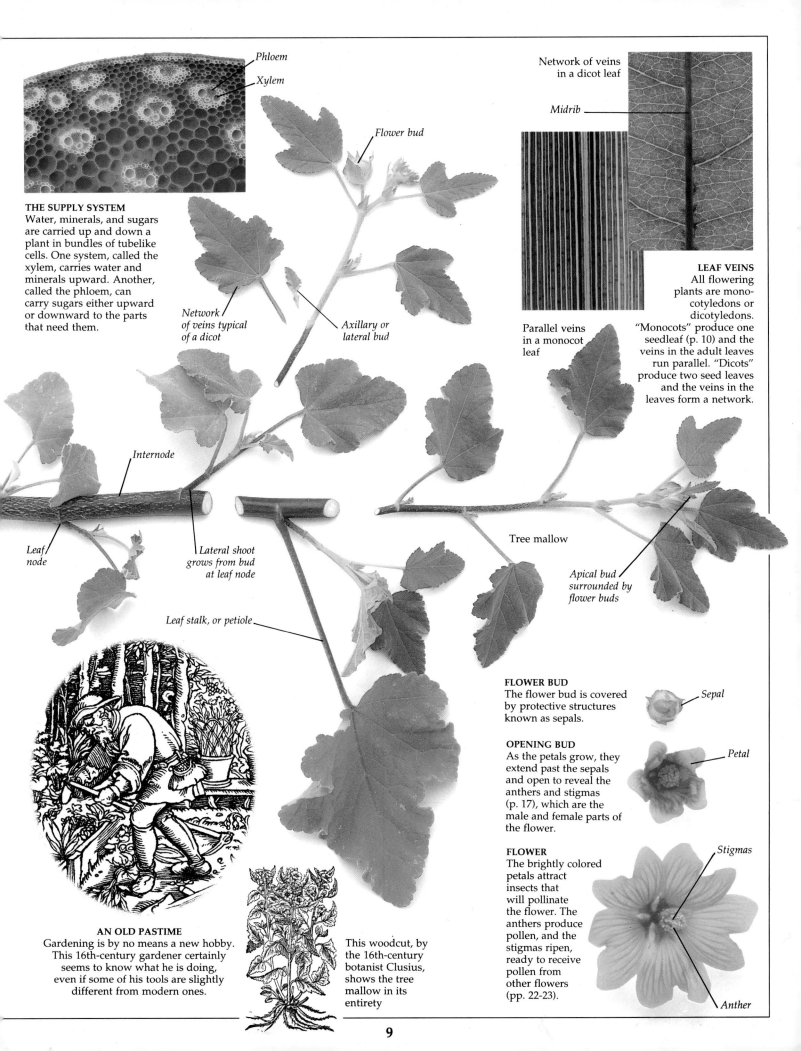

Phloem

Xylem

THE SUPPLY SYSTEM
Water, minerals, and sugars are carried up and down a plant in bundles of tubelike cells. One system, called the xylem, carries water and minerals upward. Another, called the phloem, can carry sugars either upward or downward to the parts that need them.

Network of veins typical of a dicot

Flower bud

Axillary or lateral bud

Network of veins in a dicot leaf

Midrib

LEAF VEINS
All flowering plants are mono-cotyledons or dicotyledons. "Monocots" produce one seedleaf (p. 10) and the veins in the adult leaves run parallel. "Dicots" produce two seed leaves and the veins in the leaves form a network.

Parallel veins in a monocot leaf

Internode

Leaf node

Lateral shoot grows from bud at leaf node

Tree mallow

Apical bud surrounded by flower buds

Leaf stalk, or petiole

FLOWER BUD
The flower bud is covered by protective structures known as sepals.

Sepal

OPENING BUD
As the petals grow, they extend past the sepals and open to reveal the anthers and stigmas (p. 17), which are the male and female parts of the flower.

Petal

FLOWER
The brightly colored petals attract insects that will pollinate the flower. The anthers produce pollen, and the stigmas ripen, ready to receive pollen from other flowers (pp. 22-23).

Stigmas

Anther

AN OLD PASTIME
Gardening is by no means a new hobby. This 16th-century gardener certainly seems to know what he is doing, even if some of his tools are slightly different from modern ones.

This woodcut, by the 16th-century botanist Clusius, shows the tree mallow in its entirety

9

A plant is born

A SEED IS A TINY LIFE-SUPPORT PACKAGE. Inside it is an embryo, which consists of the basic parts from which the seedling will develop, together with a supply of food. The food is needed to keep the embryo alive and fuel the process of germination (growth). It is either packed around the embryo, in an endosperm, or stored in special seed leaves, known as cotyledons. For weeks, months, or even years, the seed may remain inactive. But then, when the conditions are right, it suddenly comes alive and begins to grow. During germination the seed absorbs water, the cells of the embryo start to divide, and eventually the seed case, or testa, breaks open. First, the beginning of the root system, or radicle, sprouts and grows downward, followed rapidly by the shoot, or plumule, which will produce the stem and leaves.

First true leaves open out

Terminal bud surrounded by next pair of leaves

First true leaves

Seed coat, or testa, containing seed leaves

Bent plumule

Plumule straightens toward light

TINY BUT STRONG
When plants grow, they can exert great pressure. Some seedlings can easily push through the tar on the surface of a new road.

First roots grow downward

3 HARNESSING THE SUN
With the opening of the first true leaves, the seedling starts to produce its own food by photosynthesis (pp. 14-15). Until this time, its growth is fueled entirely by the food reserves stored in the seed leaves.

1 GETTING GOING
The seed of a scarlet runner will germinate only if it is dark and damp. First the skin of the seed splits. The beginning of the root system, the radicle, appears and grows downward. Shortly after this, a shoot appears, initially bent double with its tip buried in the seed leaves. This shoot, or plumule, will produce the stem and leaves.

2 REACHING FOR THE LIGHT
As the plumule grows longer, it breaks above ground. Once it is above the soil, it straightens up toward the light, and the first true leaves appear. In the scarlet runner, the seed leaves stay buried. This is known as "hypogeal" germination. In plants that have "epigeal" germination, such as the sunflower, the seed leaves are lifted above ground, where they turn green and start to produce food for the seedling.

Main root grows deeper

Root hairs absorb water and salts from the soil

10

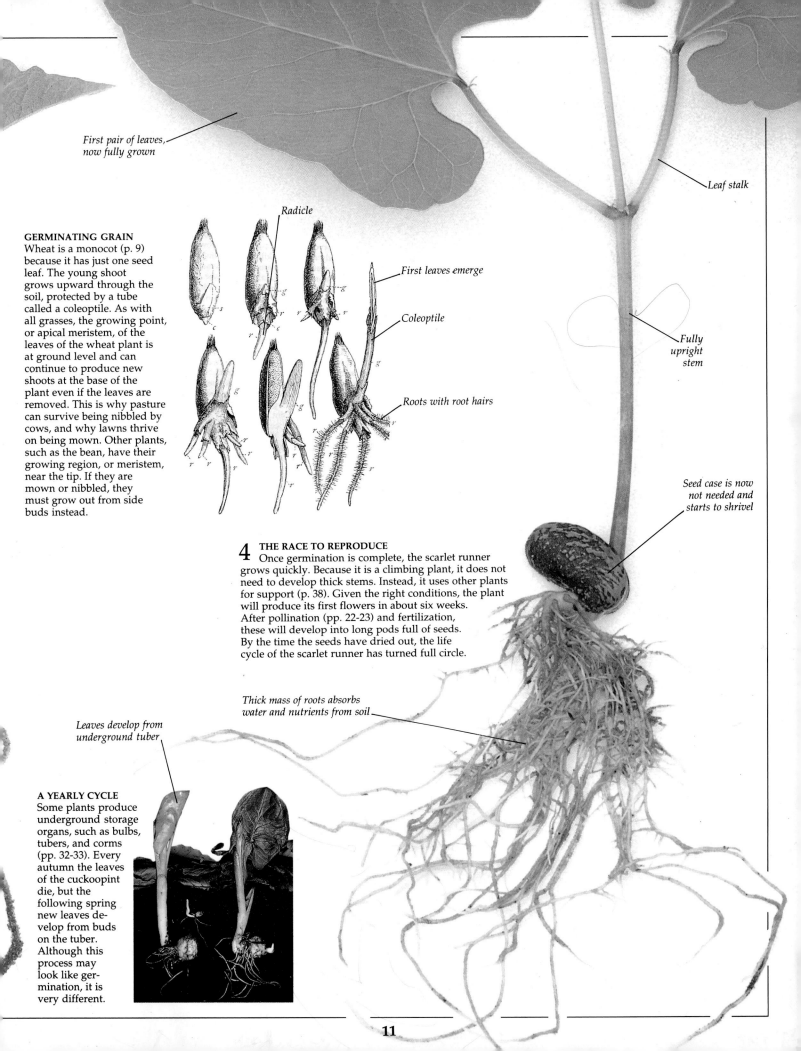

First pair of leaves, now fully grown

Leaf stalk

Radicle

First leaves emerge

Coleoptile

Roots with root hairs

Fully upright stem

Seed case is now not needed and starts to shrivel

GERMINATING GRAIN

Wheat is a monocot (p. 9) because it has just one seed leaf. The young shoot grows upward through the soil, protected by a tube called a coleoptile. As with all grasses, the growing point, or apical meristem, of the leaves of the wheat plant is at ground level and can continue to produce new shoots at the base of the plant even if the leaves are removed. This is why pasture can survive being nibbled by cows, and why lawns thrive on being mown. Other plants, such as the bean, have their growing region, or meristem, near the tip. If they are mown or nibbled, they must grow out from side buds instead.

4 THE RACE TO REPRODUCE

Once germination is complete, the scarlet runner grows quickly. Because it is a climbing plant, it does not need to develop thick stems. Instead, it uses other plants for support (p. 38). Given the right conditions, the plant will produce its first flowers in about six weeks. After pollination (pp. 22-23) and fertilization, these will develop into long pods full of seeds. By the time the seeds have dried out, the life cycle of the scarlet runner has turned full circle.

Thick mass of roots absorbs water and nutrients from soil

Leaves develop from underground tuber

A YEARLY CYCLE

Some plants produce underground storage organs, such as bulbs, tubers, and corms (pp. 32-33). Every autumn the leaves of the cuckoopint die, but the following spring new leaves develop from buds on the tuber. Although this process may look like germination, it is very different.

Bursting into bloom

PLANT LOVERS ARE OFTEN PUZZLED as to why, try as they might, they cannot get their houseplants to flower. A plant may be covered in blooms when it is bought, but the following year it will often produce nothing but a mass of green leaves. The reason is that nursery owners treat plants in a particular way to make them flower. All plants have a special control mechanism that makes sure their flowers develop and open at exactly the right time of year. The main factor in bringing a plant to bloom is the length of the night. Some plants will flower only when the nights are long and the days are short (short-day plants). The chrysanthemum, for example, will not flower at all if it is grown indoors in a position where it gets natural light by day and artificial light at night. Other plants, especially those that live far from the equator, flower only at the height of summer, when the days are long. Some flower in any day-length. Once a flower has opened, other mechanisms come into play. Many flowers turn so that they are always facing the sun; others close up every night and reopen in the morning.

Petals folded back

New petals unfolding outward

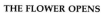

Petal *Sepal*

THE FLOWER OPENS
The garden nasturtium belongs to a family of plants that comes from South America. When the light conditions are right for the plant, flower buds begin to form. Each flower bud is protected by five sepals. As the bud starts to burst, the sepals open to reveal five bright orange petals which grow outward and fold back. One of the sepals develops a long spur which lies at the back of the flower. This spur produces the nectar that attracts insect pollinators to the flower.

BLOOMING LOVELY
Markings called honey guides show insects the way to the nectar. To reach it, they have to clamber over the anthers (p. 17), which dust them with pollen. As the days pass, the anthers wither and the three stigmas (p. 17) are ready to receive the pollen of other plants. Insects in search of nectar now dust the stigmas with pollen.

The life cycles of plants

Flowering plants have very different life spans, ranging from months to centuries. A common poppy will germinate, flower, scatter seed, and die all within a single year. Plants that live in this way are known as annuals. Other plants, such as the wild carrot (p. 55), take two years to complete the same process. They flower only in their second year - the first is spent growing and building up food reserves, which they store in a thick, fleshy root. These plants are known as biennials. Perennial plants are those that live for a number of years. They include species such as the dandelion (pp. 30-31). Perennial weeds are a particular problem for gardeners because their long life span gives them time to grow very wide-spreading roots.

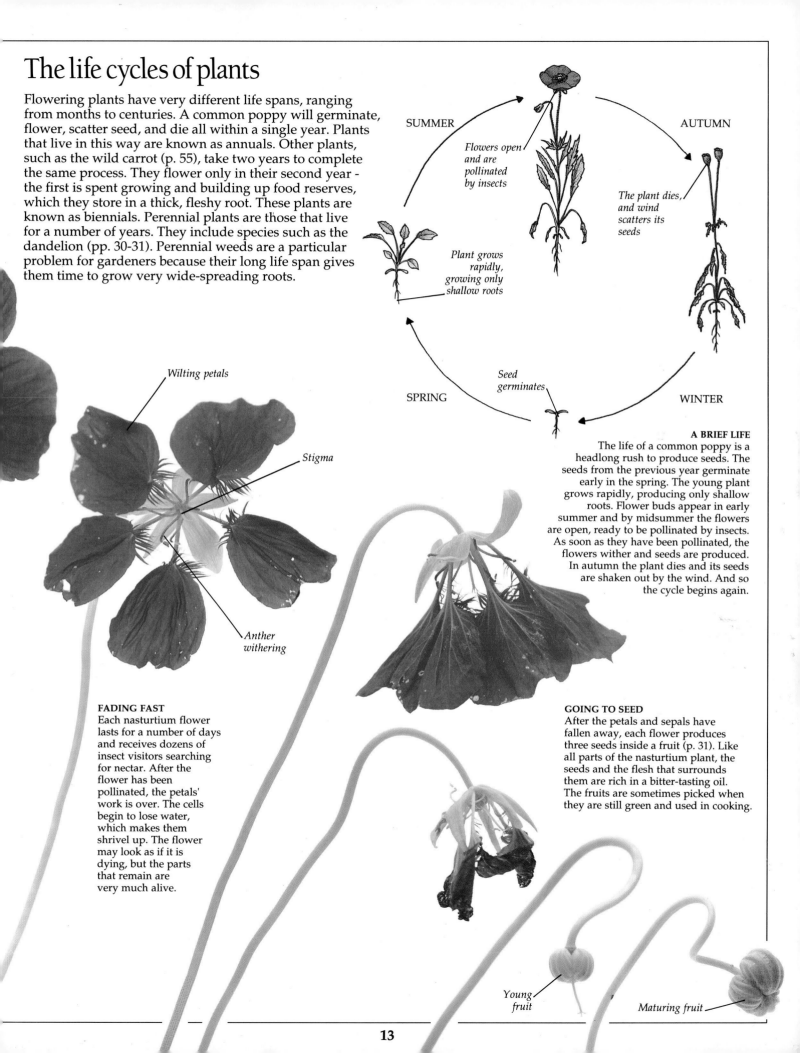

SUMMER

AUTUMN

Flowers open and are pollinated by insects

The plant dies, and wind scatters its seeds

Plant grows rapidly, growing only shallow roots

Seed germinates

SPRING

WINTER

Wilting petals

Stigma

Anther withering

A BRIEF LIFE
The life of a common poppy is a headlong rush to produce seeds. The seeds from the previous year germinate early in the spring. The young plant grows rapidly, producing only shallow roots. Flower buds appear in early summer and by midsummer the flowers are open, ready to be pollinated by insects. As soon as they have been pollinated, the flowers wither and seeds are produced. In autumn the plant dies and its seeds are shaken out by the wind. And so the cycle begins again.

FADING FAST
Each nasturtium flower lasts for a number of days and receives dozens of insect visitors searching for nectar. After the flower has been pollinated, the petals' work is over. The cells begin to lose water, which makes them shrivel up. The flower may look as if it is dying, but the parts that remain are very much alive.

GOING TO SEED
After the petals and sepals have fallen away, each flower produces three seeds inside a fruit (p. 31). Like all parts of the nasturtium plant, the seeds and the flesh that surrounds them are rich in a bitter-tasting oil. The fruits are sometimes picked when they are still green and used in cooking.

Young fruit

Maturing fruit

A light diet

UNLIKE ANIMALS, most plants do not need to find food because they can make it for themselves. The key to the way they do this lies in a green pigment called chlorophyll, which gives them their characteristic green color. By means of chlorophyll, plants can convert energy from sunlight into chemical energy which can be stored, usually in the form of starch, and used to fuel the growth and development of the plant. The light energy is used to convert carbon dioxide and water into an energy-rich food compound called glucose. This process, known as photosynthesis, works kind of like a bonfire in reverse. If you throw a log onto the fire, the carbon that is contained in compounds in the log is reconverted into carbon dioxide gas, and the stored energy is released in the form of heat and light.

UNDERGROUND STORAGE
Potatoes are swollen underground stems, known as tubers, which store the food produced by photosynthesis. This food, in the form of starches, provides the young shoots, which develop from buds on the tuber, with enough fuel to enable them to grow quickly. Potatoes also provide an important source of human food and they have been bred to produce bigger tubers.

A PLANT WITHOUT LIGHT
This potato has spent six months with very little light - a condition that would kill many plants. Because it has been in almost complete darkness, it has not been able to produce any food by photosynthesis. However, it has survived and has even produced some roots and shoots. To do this, the young potato shoots have drawn on the food reserves stored by the parent plant during the previous year's growth. The parent plant used the sun's energy to make food, which it stored in the potato tubers mostly in the form of grains of starch. The young potato plants use the starch to release energy for growth.

Leaves produced in the dark have little chlorophyll, leaving them pale, or etiolated

Potato tuber kept in dark for six months

Stems grow upward against gravity

Each stem is produced by a small bud, or eye

Adventitious roots

Tuber begins to shrink as food stores are used up

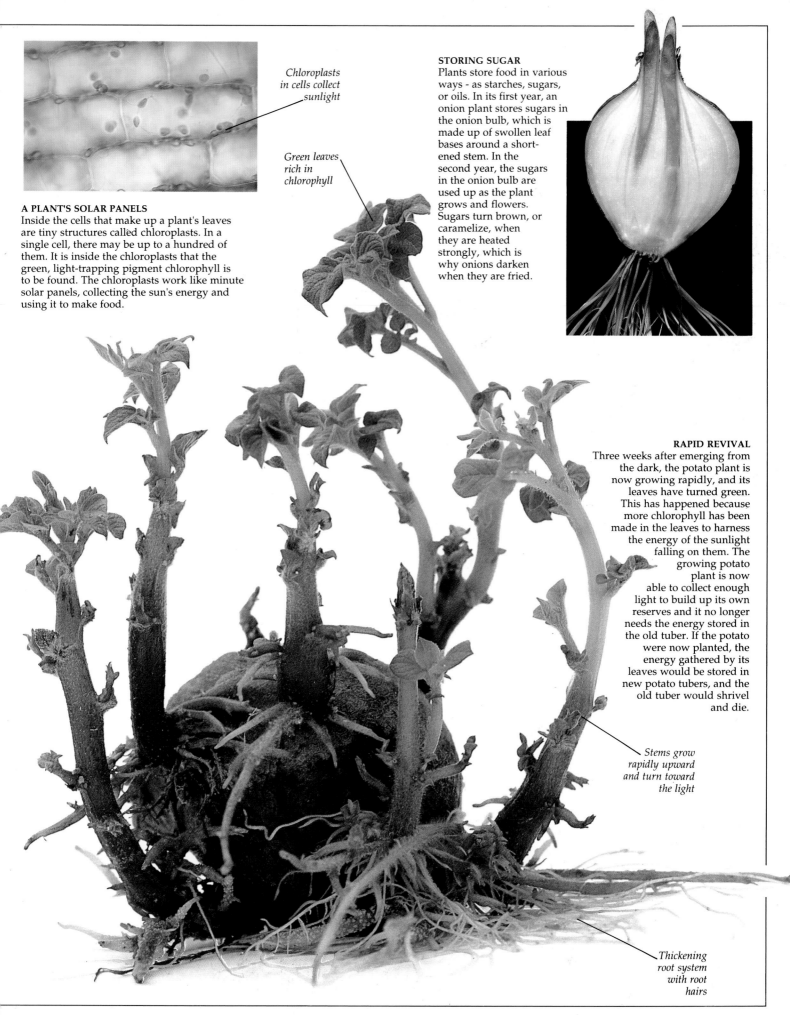

A PLANT'S SOLAR PANELS

Inside the cells that make up a plant's leaves are tiny structures called chloroplasts. In a single cell, there may be up to a hundred of them. It is inside the chloroplasts that the green, light-trapping pigment chlorophyll is to be found. The chloroplasts work like minute solar panels, collecting the sun's energy and using it to make food.

Chloroplasts in cells collect sunlight

Green leaves rich in chlorophyll

STORING SUGAR

Plants store food in various ways - as starches, sugars, or oils. In its first year, an onion plant stores sugars in the onion bulb, which is made up of swollen leaf bases around a shortened stem. In the second year, the sugars in the onion bulb are used up as the plant grows and flowers. Sugars turn brown, or caramelize, when they are heated strongly, which is why onions darken when they are fried.

RAPID REVIVAL

Three weeks after emerging from the dark, the potato plant is now growing rapidly, and its leaves have turned green. This has happened because more chlorophyll has been made in the leaves to harness the energy of the sunlight falling on them. The growing potato plant is now able to collect enough light to build up its own reserves and it no longer needs the energy stored in the old tuber. If the potato were now planted, the energy gathered by its leaves would be stored in new potato tubers, and the old tuber would shrivel and die.

Stems grow rapidly upward and turn toward the light

Thickening root system with root hairs

A simple flower dissected

FLOWERS HAVE BECOME extraordinarily varied during the course of evolution. Nature has produced them in a tremendous wealth of shapes and colors, and to add to this profusion people have bred flowers that are even more brilliant or bizarre than the ones found in the wild. But behind this baffling array of shapes and sizes there is a common pattern. For seed production, all flowers use the same underlying structures. The lily flower shown on these two pages is quite simple - its parts are all separate, and they can all be clearly seen. They fall into three groups. The male parts (the stamens) produce the pollen; the female parts (the carpel) produce the ovules, which will eventually become the seeds. Around both the male and the female parts are sepals and petals which attract insects. When, as in this lily flower, the sepals and petals look the same, they are known as perianth segments, or tepals.

The simplest flowers have the parts arranged in a circle, or whorl

Stamen

Stigma

Petal from inner whorl

Sepal from outer whorl

When sepals and petals look the same, they are known as perianth segments, or tepals

THE LILY FAMILY
The lilies and their relatives make up one of the largest families of flowering plants.

Stamens and stigma packed tightly together

Tepals protecting male and female parts of flower

HOW A FLOWER BUD OPENS
In the lily's flower bud, the male and female parts are packed tightly together inside the protective casing formed by the sepals and petals (tepals). The flower bud opens because certain parts of it start to grow more quickly than others. The inside of the base of each tepal, for example, grows faster than the outside. This forces the tepal to bend outward at the point where it is connected to the flower stalk. At the same time, unequal growth along the edges of each tepal makes the folds in it open out.

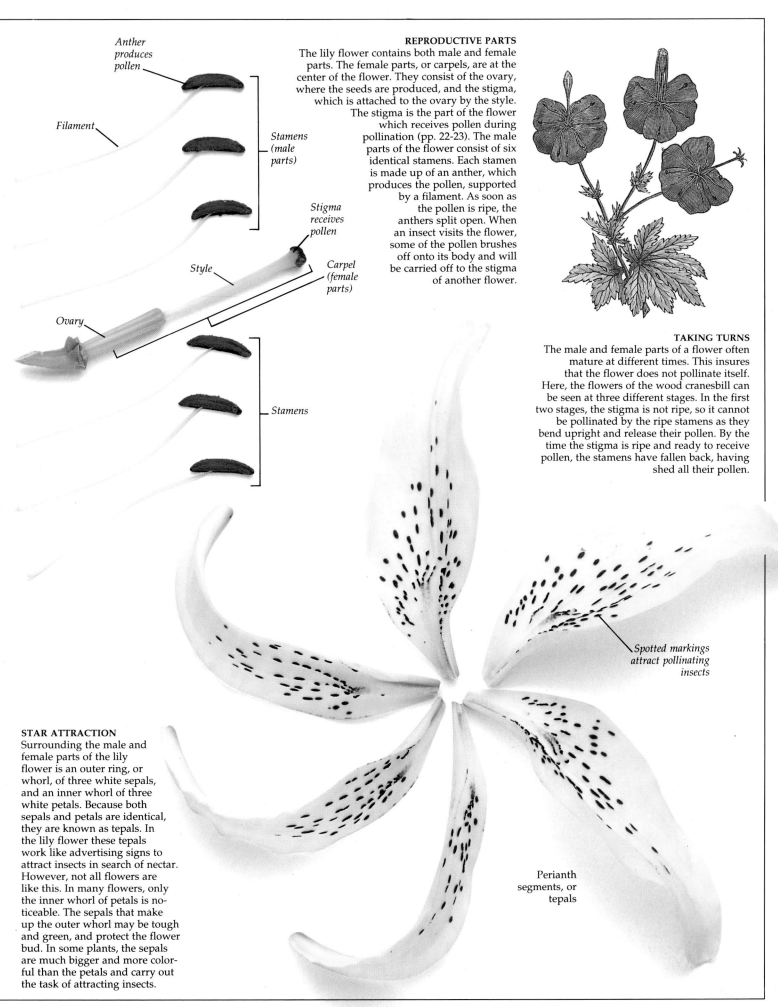

Anther
produces
pollen

Filament

Stamens
(male
parts)

Stigma
receives
pollen

Style

Carpel
(female
parts)

Ovary

Stamens

REPRODUCTIVE PARTS
The lily flower contains both male and female parts. The female parts, or carpels, are at the center of the flower. They consist of the ovary, where the seeds are produced, and the stigma, which is attached to the ovary by the style. The stigma is the part of the flower which receives pollen during pollination (pp. 22-23). The male parts of the flower consist of six identical stamens. Each stamen is made up of an anther, which produces the pollen, supported by a filament. As soon as the pollen is ripe, the anthers split open. When an insect visits the flower, some of the pollen brushes off onto its body and will be carried off to the stigma of another flower.

TAKING TURNS
The male and female parts of a flower often mature at different times. This insures that the flower does not pollinate itself. Here, the flowers of the wood cranesbill can be seen at three different stages. In the first two stages, the stigma is not ripe, so it cannot be pollinated by the ripe stamens as they bend upright and release their pollen. By the time the stigma is ripe and ready to receive pollen, the stamens have fallen back, having shed all their pollen.

Spotted markings
attract pollinating
insects

STAR ATTRACTION
Surrounding the male and female parts of the lily flower is an outer ring, or whorl, of three white sepals, and an inner whorl of three white petals. Because both sepals and petals are identical, they are known as tepals. In the lily flower these tepals work like advertising signs to attract insects in search of nectar. However, not all flowers are like this. In many flowers, only the inner whorl of petals is noticeable. The sepals that make up the outer whorl may be tough and green, and protect the flower bud. In some plants, the sepals are much bigger and more colorful than the petals and carry out the task of attracting insects.

Perianth
segments, or
tepals

A complex flower

Developing flower bud from the side

Developing nectar spur

Flowers develop in clusters and open one at a time

Pouch-shaped third sepal

Nectar spur

Front, or anterior, petal

Sepal

Stigma

Corona of threadlike hairs

Anther

Two petals joined together

THE FLOWERS on these two pages come from the Himalayan balsam. Although they have the same basic parts as the lily flower shown on pages 16-17, evolution has modified them in different ways so that the two flowers look completely different. Compared with the lily flower, the flowers of the balsam are much more complex and specialized. Himalayan balsam flowers are pollinated by long-tongued insects, such as bees, and they are shaped to insure that when the insect approaches and enters the flower, it picks up the grains of pollen from the anthers. Bees are attracted to the flower by sugary nectar which is produced in a spur attached to a pouch at the back of the flower. To reach this nectar, a visiting bee first has to land on a platform made up of petals. It then has to climb right inside the flower and stretch out its long tongue. When the bee is in this position, its back touches the anthers. These give it a dusting of pollen which it then carries to the next flower it visits.

A PAT ON THE BACK
Insects visit passionflowers in search of nectar produced in the base of the flower. When the passionflower opens, the anthers, which are lower than the styles (p. 17), dust pollen onto the insect's back. A few hours later the styles curve downward so that they are lower than the empty anthers and can collect pollen from another insect's back.

ATTRACTIVE TO INSECTS
Himalayan balsam flowers each have three sepals and five petals, and are symmetrical (even) insofar as each half is a mirror image of the other. Two of the sepals are small flaps at the base of the flower. They protect the young flower bud. During millions of years of evolution, the third has become much larger and shaped into a pouch. At the end of this pouch lies the narrow spur which produces nectar.

Fully formed flower from the side

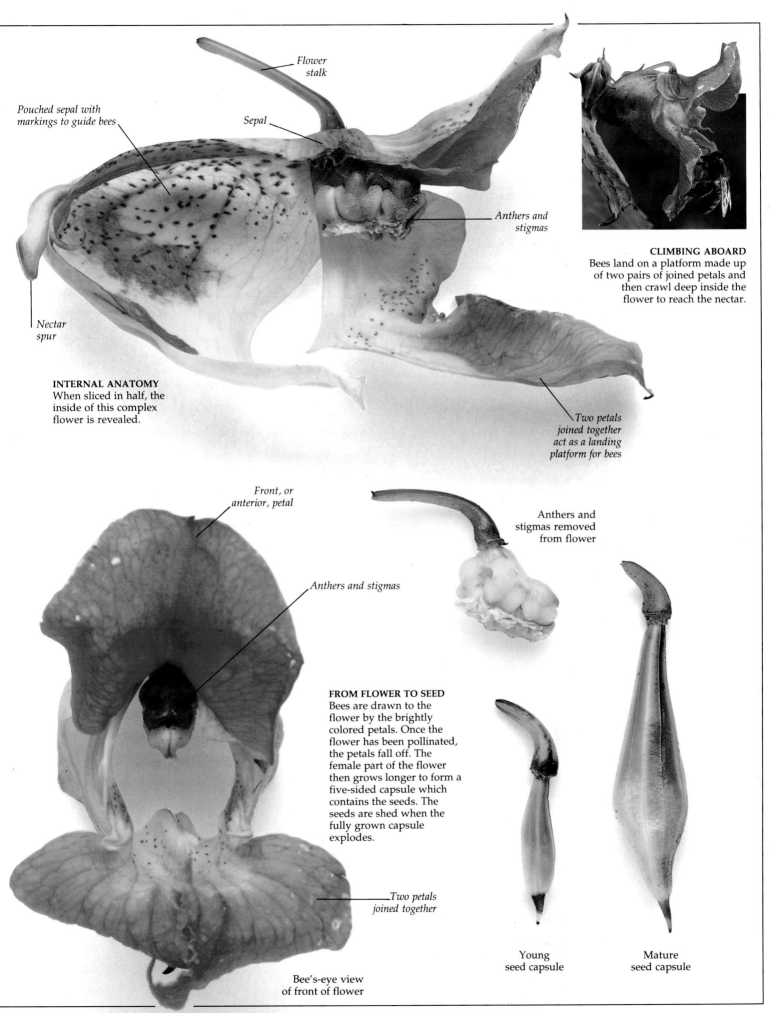

Flower stalk

Pouched sepal with markings to guide bees

Sepal

Anthers and stigmas

Nectar spur

INTERNAL ANATOMY
When sliced in half, the inside of this complex flower is revealed.

Two petals joined together act as a landing platform for bees

CLIMBING ABOARD
Bees land on a platform made up of two pairs of joined petals and then crawl deep inside the flower to reach the nectar.

Front, or anterior, petal

Anthers and stigmas

Anthers and stigmas removed from flower

FROM FLOWER TO SEED
Bees are drawn to the flower by the brightly colored petals. Once the flower has been pollinated, the petals fall off. The female part of the flower then grows longer to form a five-sided capsule which contains the seeds. The seeds are shed when the fully grown capsule explodes.

Two petals joined together

Bee's-eye view of front of flower

Young seed capsule

Mature seed capsule

All sorts of flowers

Bear's-breeches

Petals fused to form a tube

HOW MANY INDIVIDUAL FLOWERS are there on these two pages? The question is not quite as simple as it sounds. You would certainly need a magnifying glass to work out the answer, because the final figure adds up to at least 3,300. Some plants, such as the tulip, each have just a single flower. Others, like the dog rose, have a lot of flowers, but each one develops and blooms separately. Many other plants - including most of the plants on these two pages - produce flowers grouped together in clusters known as flower heads. Flower heads have many different shapes, and they vary widely in size and in the number of flowers they contain. The world's biggest individual flower, produced by the giant rafflesia (pp. 44-45), is completely dwarfed by the world's biggest flower head. This is grown by the rare South American puya, which reaches a height of nearly 33 ft (10 m).

Honeysuckle

Mullein

Fireweed

Dog rose

Individual flower

Individual flower

REGULAR FLOWERS *above*
A flower is described as being regular if all the flower parts, including the sepals, petals, anthers, and stigma, are positioned on a simple circular plan, like the dog rose above.

The rose on this Tudor coin is based on the dog rose

The iris is a regular flower that can be cut symmetrically into three pieces.

Iris

FLOWER SPIRES *left*
Flowers in spires usually open in sequence, starting at the bottom. This sequence may take a number of weeks to complete. By the time the last flower has opened, the first may have already scattered seed.

IRREGULAR FLOWERS *right*
An irregular flower is still symmetrical (even), but in a more limited way. Most irregular flowers are bi-laterally symmetrical, meaning that they can be divided into two halves that are mirror images of each other.

Sepal

Petal

Sweet pea

Clematis

SHOWY TEPALS
The sepals and petals of some flowers, like the clematis, are so similar that it is difficult to tell them apart. These parts are known as tepals (p. 16) and may be brightly colored.

Ray floret with single ray

Brightly colored tepal

NO PETALS?
The ray florets of composite flowers do not always have noticeable rays. Most species of chamomile have white rays (right), but in some varieties, although rays are present, they are difficult to see (left).

Disk florets

Eryngo

Eryngo has unusual domed flower heads

COMPOSITE FLOWERS
The flower heads of plants such as sunflowers and daisies are known as composite flowers, because they are composed of many tiny flowers clustered together. Sunflower heads have many hundreds of florets - disk florets in the center of the flower head, and ray florets, each with a single petal-like "ray," around the outer edge. In the yarrow (below), each flower head is made up of many individual disk florets. surrounded by about five ray florets. These flower heads are crowded together to form a bigger cluster with about 1,000 florets in all.

Sunflower

Ray florets

FLOWERS IN UMBELS
Not only are small flowers more visible if they are grouped together, but they also provide a better landing platform for pollinating insects. In plants of the carrot family, such as cow parsnip (right), flowers are grouped together in umbrella-shaped clusters called umbels. This family of plants is known as the umbellifers.

Flower head of cultivated yarrow

Flower head of cow parsnip

How a plant is pollinated

THE FASCINATING SHAPES and brilliant colors of many flowers have evolved over millions of years to make sure that tiny grains of pollen are carried from one plant to another. Pollen grains have to travel from the anthers to the stigma (pp. 16-17) for fertilization to occur and for seeds to be produced. Some plants are able to pollinate themselves (self-pollination), but most rely on receiving pollen from another plant of the same species (cross-pollination). Pollen may be scattered by wind or by water, but the most important pollinators are insects. Plants lure insects to their flowers with their bright colors and with food in the form of nectar. While the visiting insect feeds, pollen from the anthers is pressed on to its body, often at a particular place, such as on the back or on the head. The stigma of the flower that receives the pollen is in just the right place to collect it as the insect arrives. Some flowers are pollinated by a wide range of insects such as honeybees, bumblebees, hover flies, and butterflies. Others are more choosy and rely so heavily on a particular pollinator that no other insect species can do the job for them. Some species of yucca, for example, are pollinated only by a small moth, called the yucca moth. In return, the yucca provides the moth with food and a home.

FAMILY HOME
Worker bees bring nectar and pollen back to the hive to feed the developing young.

Pollen basket on hind leg

Honey guide

THE FLORAL FEEDING STATION
Honey guides (p. 12) on the flower guide the bee to the nectar. As the bees feed on the nectar, they also collect pollen in special baskets on their legs so it can be carried to the hive.

Bright yellow guide marks show bees where to land

Lower petal acts as landing platform

OPENING UP
The flower of the common toadflax is pollinated by bumblebees. When a visiting bee arrives, the throat of the flower is tightly closed. To reach the nectar at the back of the flower, the bee must open up the flower by pushing forward.

Nectar tube

CLIMBING IN
As the bumblebee climbs over the hump that seals the flower's throat and crawls inside in search of the nectar, it brushes against the anthers inside the top of the flower. These dust its back with pollen.

FEEDING TIME
As the bee feeds on the flower's nectar, any pollen it is already carrying is transferred from its back to the stigma, and the flower is pollinated.

22

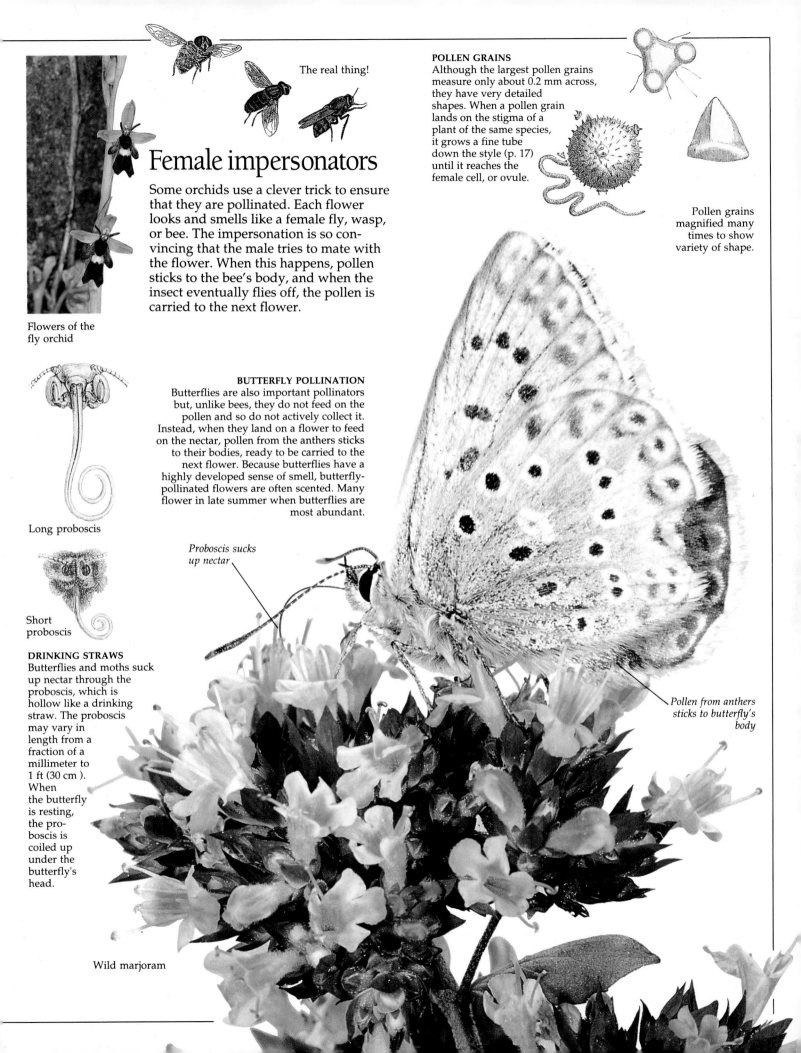

The real thing!

POLLEN GRAINS
Although the largest pollen grains measure only about 0.2 mm across, they have very detailed shapes. When a pollen grain lands on the stigma of a plant of the same species, it grows a fine tube down the style (p. 17) until it reaches the female cell, or ovule.

Pollen grains magnified many times to show variety of shape.

Female impersonators

Some orchids use a clever trick to ensure that they are pollinated. Each flower looks and smells like a female fly, wasp, or bee. The impersonation is so convincing that the male tries to mate with the flower. When this happens, pollen sticks to the bee's body, and when the insect eventually flies off, the pollen is carried to the next flower.

Flowers of the fly orchid

Long proboscis

Short proboscis

BUTTERFLY POLLINATION
Butterflies are also important pollinators but, unlike bees, they do not feed on the pollen and so do not actively collect it. Instead, when they land on a flower to feed on the nectar, pollen from the anthers sticks to their bodies, ready to be carried to the next flower. Because butterflies have a highly developed sense of smell, butterfly-pollinated flowers are often scented. Many flower in late summer when butterflies are most abundant.

Proboscis sucks up nectar

Pollen from anthers sticks to butterfly's body

DRINKING STRAWS
Butterflies and moths suck up nectar through the proboscis, which is hollow like a drinking straw. The proboscis may vary in length from a fraction of a millimeter to 1 ft (30 cm). When the butterfly is resting, the proboscis is coiled up under the butterfly's head.

Wild marjoram

Strange pollinators

Many flowers are pollinated by bees and butterflies (pp. 22-23), but some plant species depend on quite different creatures for pollination. Some are pollinated by the sort of flies that are attracted by the smell of decay. Others rely on birds, which are attracted to the flowers by bright colors and the sweet smell of nectar. Many plants are highly adapted for specific pollinators. The list of these species includes not only insects and birds, but also bats, mice, possums, and even slugs.

POLLINATION UNDERGROUND
Some orchids in Australia grow and flower underground, where they live on the decaying remains of other plants. The picture on the left shows the flower of one of these species. These flowers are most probably pollinated by a soil-dwelling creature, although it is not yet known exactly which one.

Hairs on petals attract insects

Flowers are lilac at first, but turn red as they open

Pink bracts attract birds

Shiny surface

Cultivated fly-pollinated orchid

Flowers appear among bracts

Urn plant

A LURE FOR FLIES
Bees are attracted to flowers that have a sweet smell. Many flies, on the other hand, are attracted by the smell of decaying flesh. For this reason, many flowers that rely on flies for pollination have a putrid odor. Some flowers, such as this orchid, have hairs on the surface of their petals to give them an animal-like feel. The shiny surface also attracts flies.

THE RED SIGNAL
Plants that are pollinated by birds often have red or pink petals or flower heads. Most birds have excellent color vision, and a bright red flower, which also produces nectar, readily attracts them. Because this urn plant lives high up on trees (p. 46), it needs to be noticeable to attract the attention of the bird pollinators. Most insects, apart from some butterflies, cannot see red, so it is an unusual color for insect-pollinated flowers.

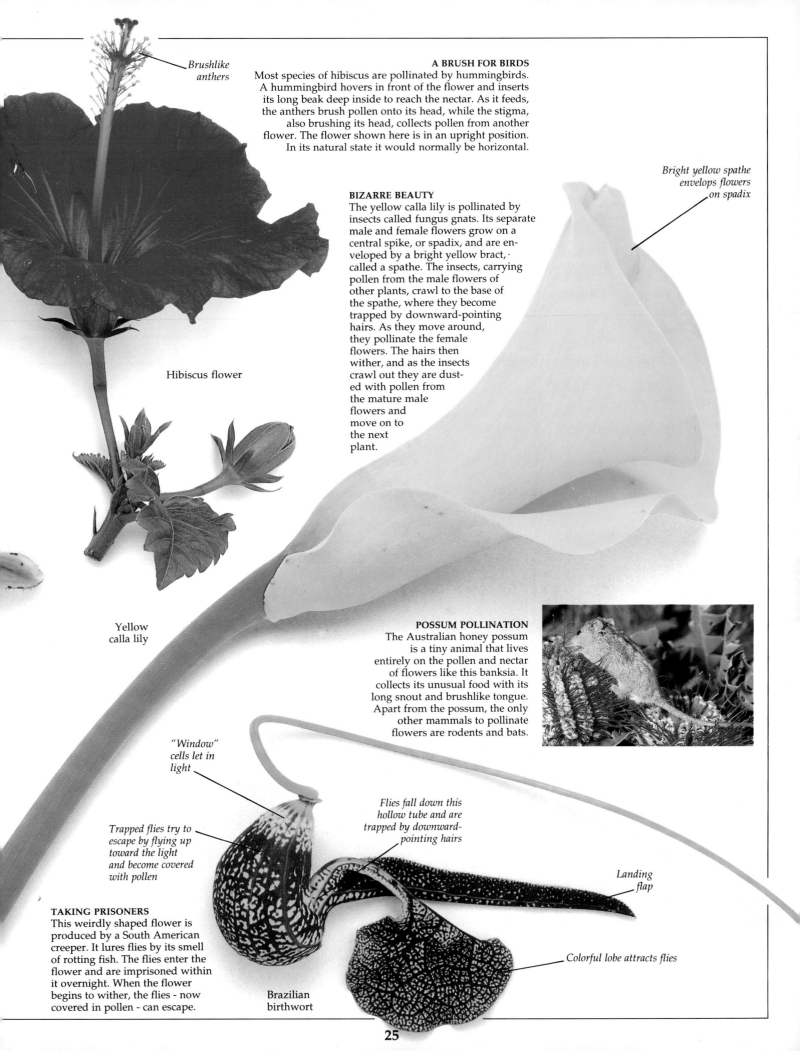

Brushlike anthers

A BRUSH FOR BIRDS
Most species of hibiscus are pollinated by hummingbirds. A hummingbird hovers in front of the flower and inserts its long beak deep inside to reach the nectar. As it feeds, the anthers brush pollen onto its head, while the stigma, also brushing its head, collects pollen from another flower. The flower shown here is in an upright position. In its natural state it would normally be horizontal.

Bright yellow spathe envelops flowers on spadix

BIZARRE BEAUTY
The yellow calla lily is pollinated by insects called fungus gnats. Its separate male and female flowers grow on a central spike, or spadix, and are enveloped by a bright yellow bract, called a spathe. The insects, carrying pollen from the male flowers of other plants, crawl to the base of the spathe, where they become trapped by downward-pointing hairs. As they move around, they pollinate the female flowers. The hairs then wither, and as the insects crawl out they are dusted with pollen from the mature male flowers and move on to the next plant.

Hibiscus flower

Yellow calla lily

POSSUM POLLINATION
The Australian honey possum is a tiny animal that lives entirely on the pollen and nectar of flowers like this banksia. It collects its unusual food with its long snout and brushlike tongue. Apart from the possum, the only other mammals to pollinate flowers are rodents and bats.

"Window" cells let in light

Flies fall down this hollow tube and are trapped by downward-pointing hairs

Trapped flies try to escape by flying up toward the light and become covered with pollen

Landing flap

TAKING PRISONERS
This weirdly shaped flower is produced by a South American creeper. It lures flies by its smell of rotting fish. The flies enter the flower and are imprisoned within it overnight. When the flower begins to wither, the flies - now covered in pollen - can escape.

Brazilian birthwort

Colorful lobe attracts flies

25

From flower to fruit

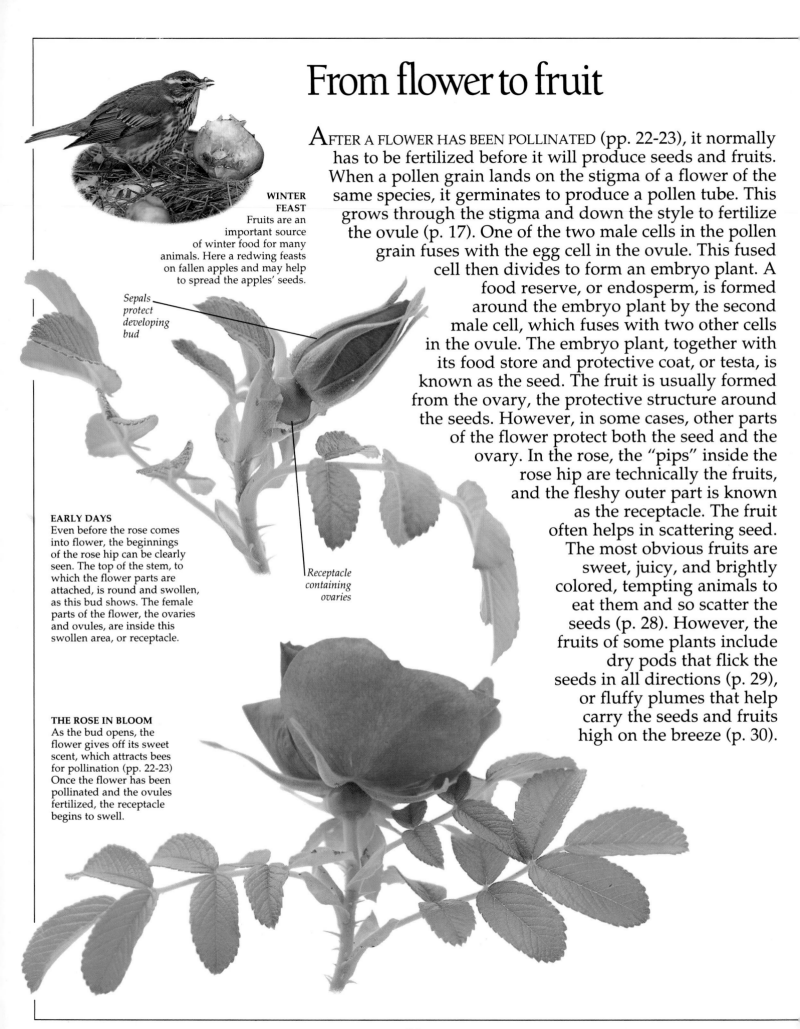

AFTER A FLOWER HAS BEEN POLLINATED (pp. 22-23), it normally has to be fertilized before it will produce seeds and fruits. When a pollen grain lands on the stigma of a flower of the same species, it germinates to produce a pollen tube. This grows through the stigma and down the style to fertilize the ovule (p. 17). One of the two male cells in the pollen grain fuses with the egg cell in the ovule. This fused cell then divides to form an embryo plant. A food reserve, or endosperm, is formed around the embryo plant by the second male cell, which fuses with two other cells in the ovule. The embryo plant, together with its food store and protective coat, or testa, is known as the seed. The fruit is usually formed from the ovary, the protective structure around the seeds. However, in some cases, other parts of the flower protect both the seed and the ovary. In the rose, the "pips" inside the rose hip are technically the fruits, and the fleshy outer part is known as the receptacle. The fruit often helps in scattering seed. The most obvious fruits are sweet, juicy, and brightly colored, tempting animals to eat them and so scatter the seeds (p. 28). However, the fruits of some plants include dry pods that flick the seeds in all directions (p. 29), or fluffy plumes that help carry the seeds and fruits high on the breeze (p. 30).

WINTER FEAST
Fruits are an important source of winter food for many animals. Here a redwing feasts on fallen apples and may help to spread the apples' seeds.

Sepals protect developing bud

Receptacle containing ovaries

EARLY DAYS
Even before the rose comes into flower, the beginnings of the rose hip can be clearly seen. The top of the stem, to which the flower parts are attached, is round and swollen, as this bud shows. The female parts of the flower, the ovaries and ovules, are inside this swollen area, or receptacle.

THE ROSE IN BLOOM
As the bud opens, the flower gives off its sweet scent, which attracts bees for pollination (pp. 22-23) Once the flower has been pollinated and the ovules fertilized, the receptacle begins to swell.

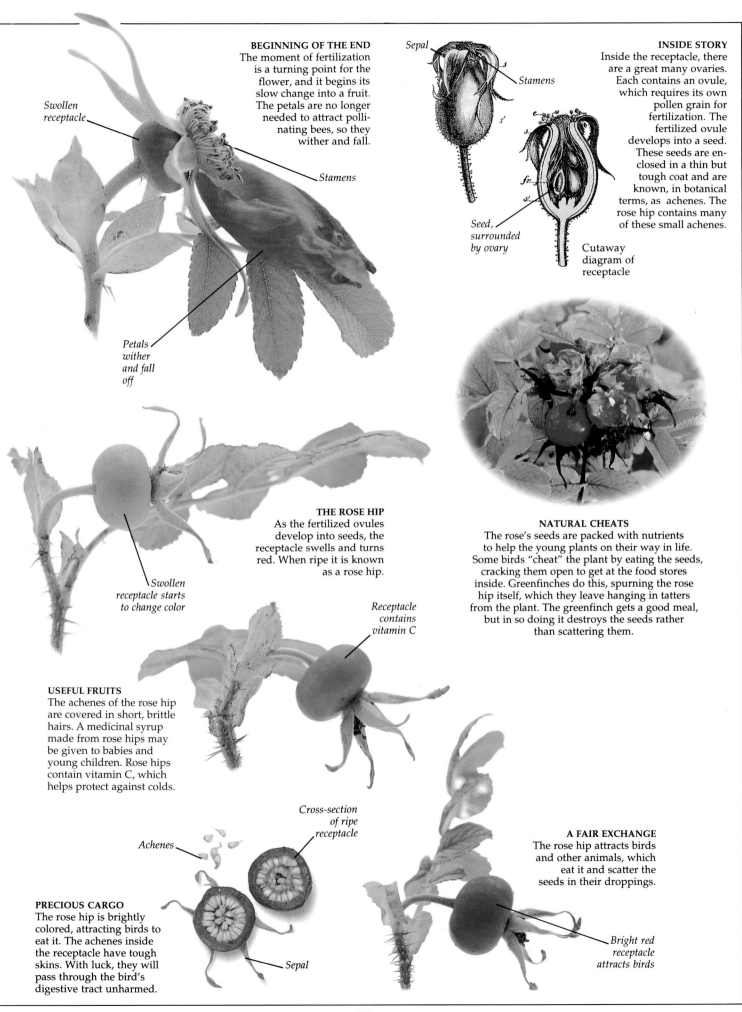

BEGINNING OF THE END
The moment of fertilization is a turning point for the flower, and it begins its slow change into a fruit. The petals are no longer needed to attract pollinating bees, so they wither and fall.

Swollen receptacle

Stamens

Petals wither and fall off

Sepal

Stamens

Seed, surrounded by ovary

Cutaway diagram of receptacle

INSIDE STORY
Inside the receptacle, there are a great many ovaries. Each contains an ovule, which requires its own pollen grain for fertilization. The fertilized ovule develops into a seed. These seeds are enclosed in a thin but tough coat and are known, in botanical terms, as achenes. The rose hip contains many of these small achenes.

THE ROSE HIP
As the fertilized ovules develop into seeds, the receptacle swells and turns red. When ripe it is known as a rose hip.

Swollen receptacle starts to change color

NATURAL CHEATS
The rose's seeds are packed with nutrients to help the young plants on their way in life. Some birds "cheat" the plant by eating the seeds, cracking them open to get at the food stores inside. Greenfinches do this, spurning the rose hip itself, which they leave hanging in tatters from the plant. The greenfinch gets a good meal, but in so doing it destroys the seeds rather than scattering them.

USEFUL FRUITS
The achenes of the rose hip are covered in short, brittle hairs. A medicinal syrup made from rose hips may be given to babies and young children. Rose hips contain vitamin C, which helps protect against colds.

Receptacle contains vitamin C

Cross-section of ripe receptacle

Achenes

A FAIR EXCHANGE
The rose hip attracts birds and other animals, which eat it and scatter the seeds in their droppings.

PRECIOUS CARGO
The rose hip is brightly colored, attracting birds to eat it. The achenes inside the receptacle have tough skins. With luck, they will pass through the bird's digestive tract unharmed.

Sepal

Bright red receptacle attracts birds

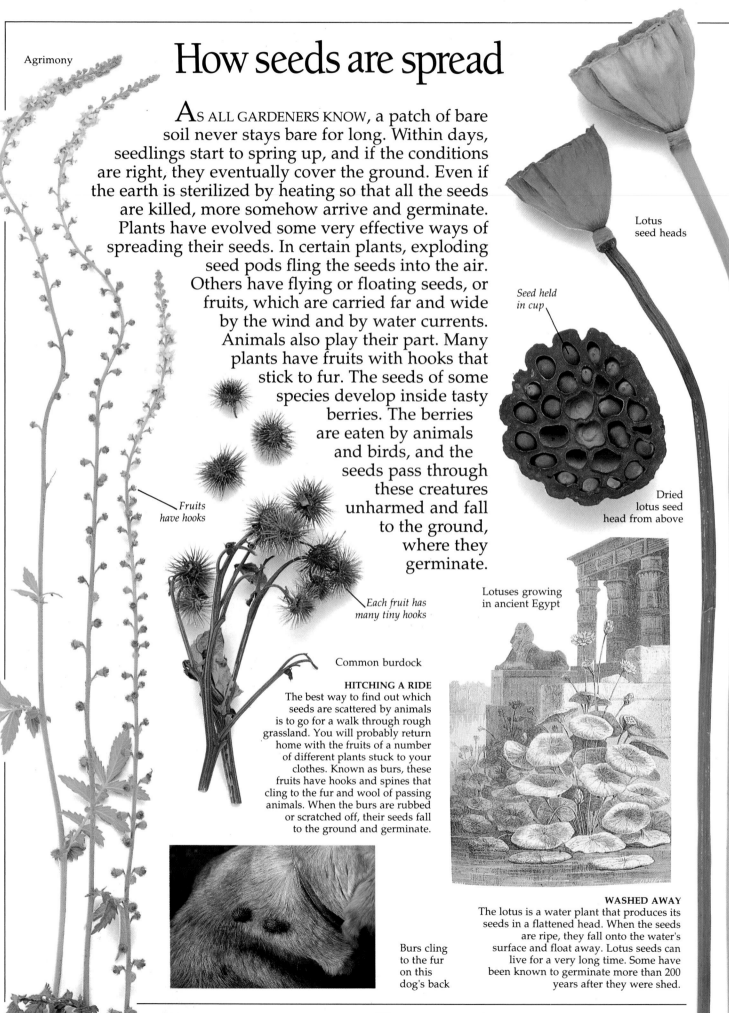

How seeds are spread

As ALL GARDENERS KNOW, a patch of bare soil never stays bare for long. Within days, seedlings start to spring up, and if the conditions are right, they eventually cover the ground. Even if the earth is sterilized by heating so that all the seeds are killed, more somehow arrive and germinate. Plants have evolved some very effective ways of spreading their seeds. In certain plants, exploding seed pods fling the seeds into the air. Others have flying or floating seeds, or fruits, which are carried far and wide by the wind and by water currents. Animals also play their part. Many plants have fruits with hooks that stick to fur. The seeds of some species develop inside tasty berries. The berries are eaten by animals and birds, and the seeds pass through these creatures unharmed and fall to the ground, where they germinate.

Agrimony

Fruits have hooks

Each fruit has many tiny hooks

Common burdock

Lotus seed heads

Seed held in cup

Dried lotus seed head from above

Lotuses growing in ancient Egypt

HITCHING A RIDE
The best way to find out which seeds are scattered by animals is to go for a walk through rough grassland. You will probably return home with the fruits of a number of different plants stuck to your clothes. Known as burs, these fruits have hooks and spines that cling to the fur and wool of passing animals. When the burs are rubbed or scratched off, their seeds fall to the ground and germinate.

Burs cling to the fur on this dog's back

WASHED AWAY
The lotus is a water plant that produces its seeds in a flattened head. When the seeds are ripe, they fall onto the water's surface and float away. Lotus seeds can live for a very long time. Some have been known to germinate more than 200 years after they were shed.

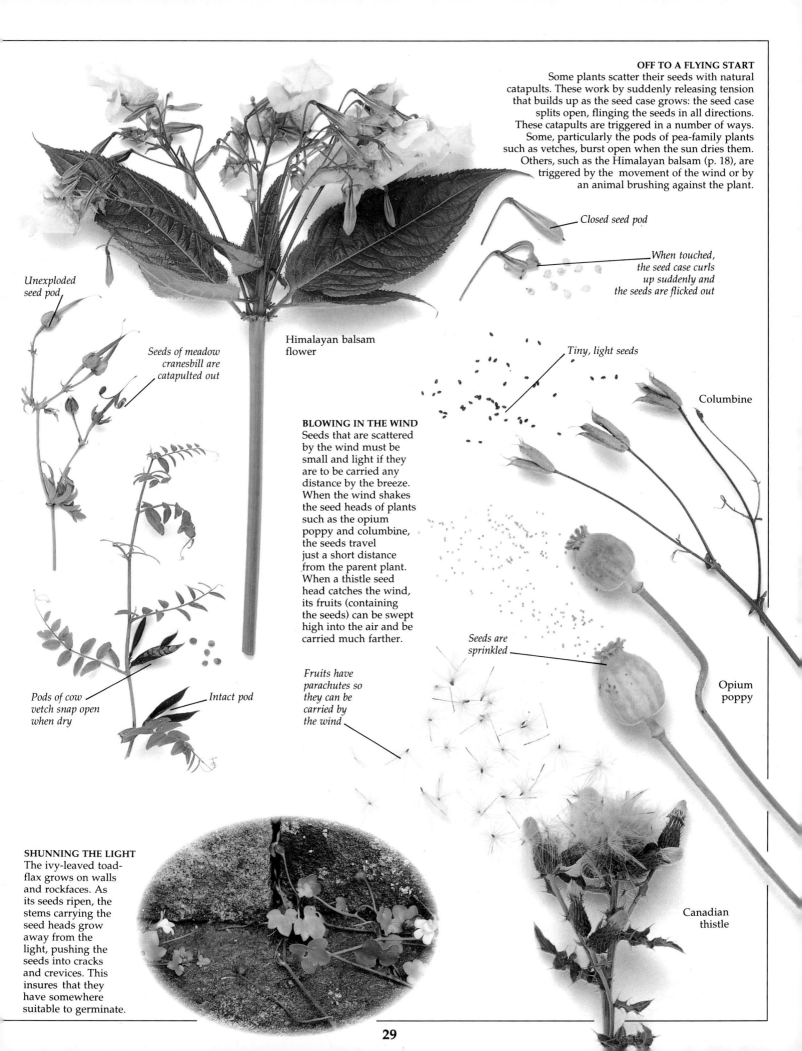

OFF TO A FLYING START
Some plants scatter their seeds with natural catapults. These work by suddenly releasing tension that builds up as the seed case grows: the seed case splits open, flinging the seeds in all directions. These catapults are triggered in a number of ways. Some, particularly the pods of pea-family plants such as vetches, burst open when the sun dries them. Others, such as the Himalayan balsam (p. 18), are triggered by the movement of the wind or by an animal brushing against the plant.

Closed seed pod

When touched, the seed case curls up suddenly and the seeds are flicked out

Unexploded seed pod

Seeds of meadow cranesbill are catapulted out

Himalayan balsam flower

Tiny, light seeds

Columbine

BLOWING IN THE WIND
Seeds that are scattered by the wind must be small and light if they are to be carried any distance by the breeze. When the wind shakes the seed heads of plants such as the opium poppy and columbine, the seeds travel just a short distance from the parent plant. When a thistle seed head catches the wind, its fruits (containing the seeds) can be swept high into the air and be carried much farther.

Seeds are sprinkled

Fruits have parachutes so they can be carried by the wind

Pods of cow vetch snap open when dry

Intact pod

Opium poppy

SHUNNING THE LIGHT
The ivy-leaved toad-flax grows on walls and rockfaces. As its seeds ripen, the stems carrying the seed heads grow away from the light, pushing the seeds into cracks and crevices. This insures that they have somewhere suitable to germinate.

Canadian thistle

Borne on the wind

ACCORDING TO TRADITION, if you make a wish and then blow on a dandelion's seed head, your wish will come true if all the seeds blow away in one puff. Whether or not the wish ever comes true, the custom certainly helps the plant to spread. The seeds of the dandelion are encased in tiny fruits and have their own special feathery parachutes to help them float through the air. If you blow on them, you may be starting the seeds on a journey that takes them high up and far away. The dandelion's flower, like that of the sunflower (p. 21), is actually a composite flower head made up of many tiny florets. Each of the florets produces a single fruit. Like the dandelion, many other composite plants, such as hawkweeds, ragworts, and thistles, rely on the wind to scatter their seeds. The fruits of some of these have parachutes; others have fine hairs that stick out in all directions to form a feathery ball. Many of these plants are troublesome weeds because they quickly colonize bare soil in gardens and on farmland.

Dandelion's tiny
fruits float away
on the breeze

1 OPENING TIME
The dandelion's flower opens in the morning and closes in the afternoon or when it rains. The plant's name comes from the French *dent de lion,* meaning lion's tooth, which describes the jagged edges of the leaves.

*Flower closes before
seeds form*

*Flower head
open, waiting to
be pollinated by
a passing insect*

2 THE SEEDS START TO FORM
After opening and closing for a number of days, during which time it may be pollinated, the flower finally closes, and seed formation begins. Gradually the yellow petals wither away, and the "pappus," which is the name given to the small circle of hairs attached to the top of each fruit, starts to grow longer. This is the beginning of the parachute.

*Bracts (specialized
leaves) protect
developing seed head*

Seed head opens when parachutes are formed

Bracts fold back

Fully opened seed head

3 **OPENING OUT**
The seed head begins to open only when the weather is dry. At first, the parachutes are squashed together, but as the bracts around the edge of the seed head fold back, the parachutes begin to expand.

4 **READY TO GO**
If the air is still, the fruits may spend several days attached to the seed head. This is a dangerous time for them, because gold-finches and other seed-eating birds are likely to peck them off and eat them.

Parachutes attached to tiny fruits

5 **LIFTOFF**
A slight breeze is all that is needed to lift the parachutes into the air. They may fall nearby, but if there is enough updraft they can be carried for long distances. When a fruit lands, it no longer needs the parachute that has carried it on its journey, and this breaks off. Over the winter the seed sinks into the soil, waiting for the spring when it will germinate.

Spreading without seeds

Creeping crowfoot

PLANTS CAN REPRODUCE in two quite different ways. As well as reproducing by means of seeds, they can sometimes also turn small pieces of themselves into new plants. This is known as vegetative reproduction. When a plant reproduces in this way, the young plantlets are genetically identical to the parent. This is quite different from reproduction with seeds, which produce seedlings that are all slightly different from their parents. Vegetative reproduction is very useful for farmers and gardeners. It means that they can multiply a plant that has attractive flowers or tasty fruit, knowing that each young plant will have exactly the characteristics they want. Some of the oldest plants in the world are reproduced by this process, like creosote plant "clones" in California. Each clone is created when a single creosote bush begins to spread by producing young plants connected to it. The original creosote bush at the center, which began life about 10,000 years ago, is now long dead, but its clones are still alive and spreading today.

Piggyback plant

THE PIGGYBACK PLANT
The piggyback plant has an unusual way of reproducing. Tiny new plantlets grow at the base of the older leaves and look as though they are having a piggyback ride.

Parent plant

CREEPING STEMS
Some plants, such as the creeping crowfoot, spread by means of stolons, which are leafy stems that grow along the ground. When the stolons reach a certain length, a new, young plant develops from a bud at the leaf node (p. 9) and the stolon eventually withers away completely.

Strawberry plant

Parent plant

Fallen plantlets

Stolon, or runner

Bud at leaf node

Chandelier plant

PLANTLETS AT LEAF TIPS
Kalanchoes are succulents (p. 53), many of which reproduce by developing tiny plantlets along the edges of their leaves. Others, like this chandelier plant, have them just at the tips. When a plantlet is mature, it falls off the parent plant and takes root in the soil beneath.

STRAWBERRY RUNNERS
After they have fruited, strawberry plants produce long stolons known as runners which spread out over the ground. Strawberry growers wait until the young plants have rooted and then cut the runners. The new plants can be transplanted to make a new strawberry bed.

A MYTH EXPLODED
The famous tumbleweed of the western prairies is uprooted by strong winds after it has flowered and is often blown far away from the place where it grew. Because it is dead, the plant cannot put down roots once it comes to a halt, as is often supposed. Instead, it spreads by seeds. The plant scatters them as it tumbles along the ground.

Iris rhizome

Tuber of Jerusalem artichoke

RHIZOMES
A rhizome is a usually horizontal stem produced by a perennial plant (p. 13), either underground or on the surface. As the rhizome spreads, it occasionally divides, producing roots, stems, and leaves. The oldest part of the rhizome may die away so that these new shoots form separate plants.

Iris

Stolon

TUBERS
Tubers are swollen underground stems. They store food to produce new plants and also to help the parent plant survive in difficult conditions. When gardeners and farmers uproot tuber crops like potatoes, they have to be careful to dig up every one. If even part of the potato is left in the ground, it will sprout to produce a new plant the following spring.

Tuber of potato

Young plant forming at tip of stolon

Young plant grows from a bud at the leaf node

Tulip bulb

Runner

BULBS
A bulb consists of a bud surrounded by short, very swollen leaves, with flattened underground stems. Some bulbs, such as the tulip, produce one or more new bulbs around its base every year. These can be broken off the parent bulb to form new plants.

New bulbs form around the base of the old bulb

LEAVES THAT TAKE ROOT
Plants that live in dry places often have fleshy leaves that are full of water. If these leaves are broken off, they can survive for a long time because they do not dry out as quickly as normal, thin leaves. While they are lying on the ground, many of them can put down roots and develop into new plants.

Crassula nealana

BULBS ABOVE AND BELOW GROUND
This species of onion has both bulbs and bulbils, small bulblike structures that form above ground in place of flowers.

Bulbils may fall to the ground and take root

Fleshy leaves can root themselves

Christmas-cheer

Top of plant

Bulb underground

Allium paradoxum

33

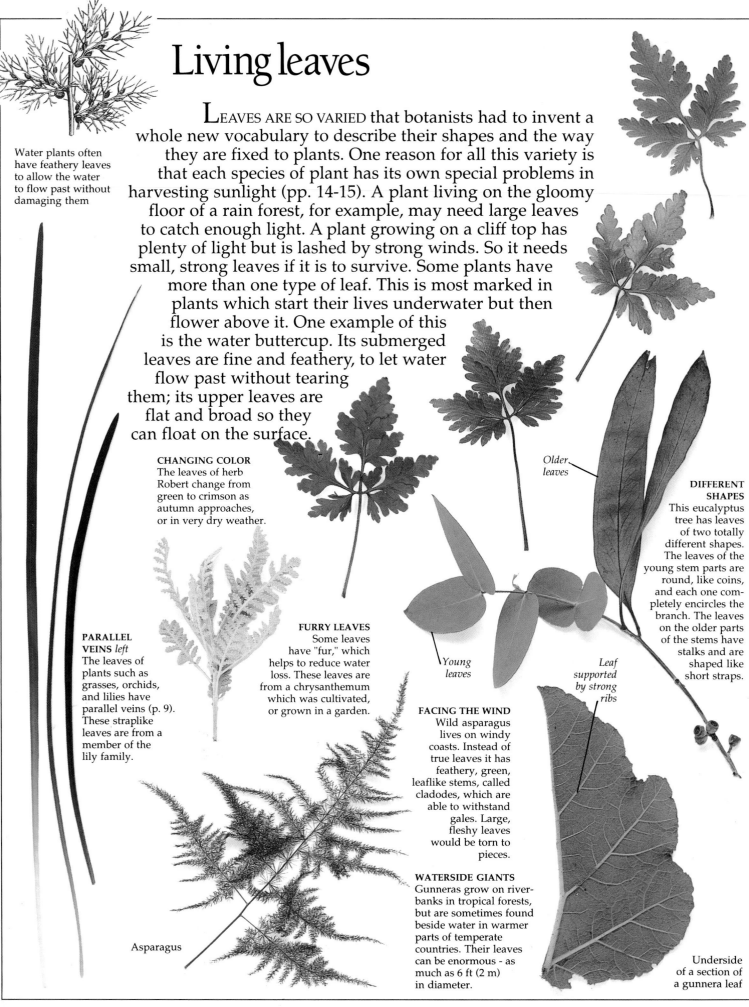

Living leaves

LEAVES ARE SO VARIED that botanists had to invent a whole new vocabulary to describe their shapes and the way they are fixed to plants. One reason for all this variety is that each species of plant has its own special problems in harvesting sunlight (pp. 14-15). A plant living on the gloomy floor of a rain forest, for example, may need large leaves to catch enough light. A plant growing on a cliff top has plenty of light but is lashed by strong winds. So it needs small, strong leaves if it is to survive. Some plants have more than one type of leaf. This is most marked in plants which start their lives underwater but then flower above it. One example of this is the water buttercup. Its submerged leaves are fine and feathery, to let water flow past without tearing them; its upper leaves are flat and broad so they can float on the surface.

Water plants often have feathery leaves to allow the water to flow past without damaging them

CHANGING COLOR
The leaves of herb Robert change from green to crimson as autumn approaches, or in very dry weather.

PARALLEL VEINS *left*
The leaves of plants such as grasses, orchids, and lilies have parallel veins (p. 9). These straplike leaves are from a member of the lily family.

FURRY LEAVES
Some leaves have "fur," which helps to reduce water loss. These leaves are from a chrysanthemum which was cultivated, or grown in a garden.

Asparagus

FACING THE WIND
Wild asparagus lives on windy coasts. Instead of true leaves it has feathery, green, leaflike stems, called cladodes, which are able to withstand gales. Large, fleshy leaves would be torn to pieces.

WATERSIDE GIANTS
Gunneras grow on riverbanks in tropical forests, but are sometimes found beside water in warmer parts of temperate countries. Their leaves can be enormous - as much as 6 ft (2 m) in diameter.

Older leaves

DIFFERENT SHAPES
This eucalyptus tree has leaves of two totally different shapes. The leaves of the young stem parts are round, like coins, and each one completely encircles the branch. The leaves on the older parts of the stems have stalks and are shaped like short straps.

Young leaves

Leaf supported by strong ribs

Underside of a section of a gunnera leaf

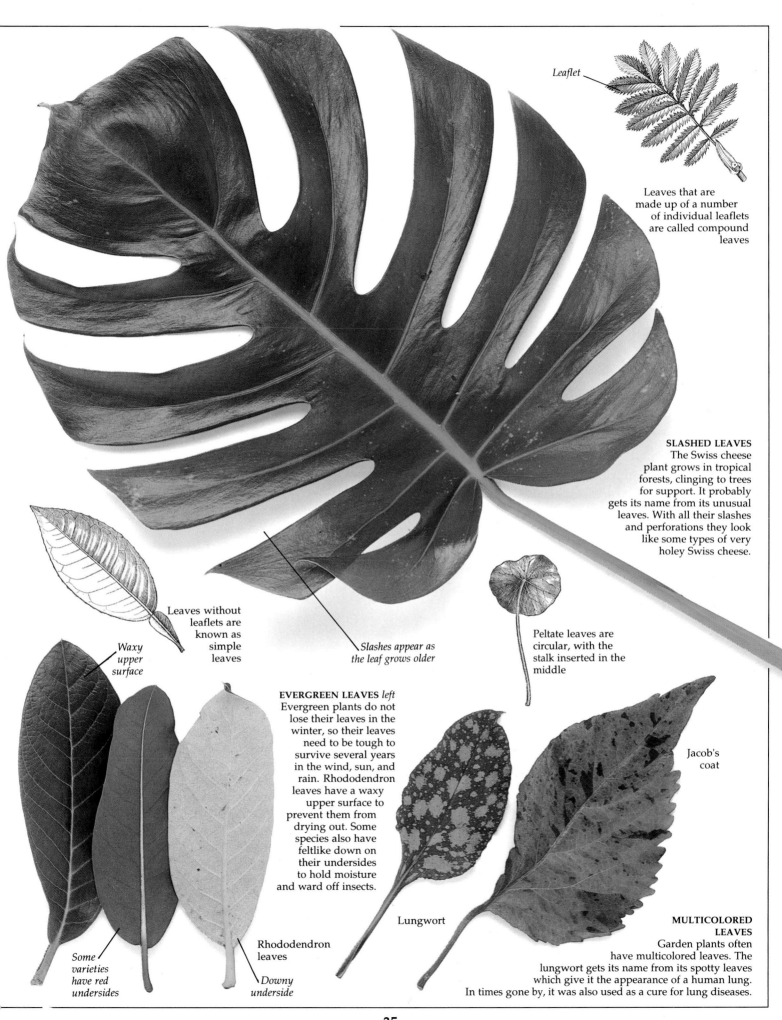

Leaflet

Leaves that are made up of a number of individual leaflets are called compound leaves

SLASHED LEAVES
The Swiss cheese plant grows in tropical forests, clinging to trees for support. It probably gets its name from its unusual leaves. With all their slashes and perforations they look like some types of very holey Swiss cheese.

Leaves without leaflets are known as simple leaves

Waxy upper surface

Slashes appear as the leaf grows older

Peltate leaves are circular, with the stalk inserted in the middle

EVERGREEN LEAVES left
Evergreen plants do not lose their leaves in the winter, so their leaves need to be tough to survive several years in the wind, sun, and rain. Rhododendron leaves have a waxy upper surface to prevent them from drying out. Some species also have feltlike down on their undersides to hold moisture and ward off insects.

Jacob's coat

Lungwort

Some varieties have red undersides

Rhododendron leaves

Downy underside

MULTICOLORED LEAVES
Garden plants often have multicolored leaves. The lungwort gets its name from its spotty leaves which give it the appearance of a human lung. In times gone by, it was also used as a cure for lung diseases.

Self-defense

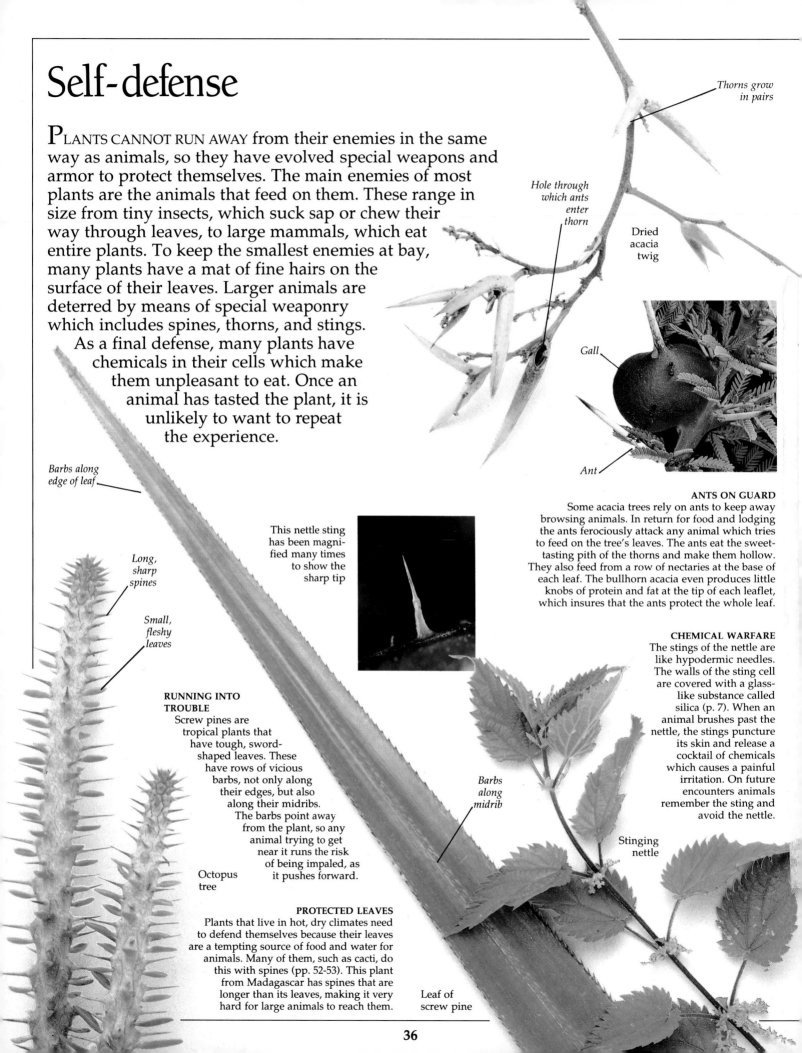

PLANTS CANNOT RUN AWAY from their enemies in the same way as animals, so they have evolved special weapons and armor to protect themselves. The main enemies of most plants are the animals that feed on them. These range in size from tiny insects, which suck sap or chew their way through leaves, to large mammals, which eat entire plants. To keep the smallest enemies at bay, many plants have a mat of fine hairs on the surface of their leaves. Larger animals are deterred by means of special weaponry which includes spines, thorns, and stings. As a final defense, many plants have chemicals in their cells which make them unpleasant to eat. Once an animal has tasted the plant, it is unlikely to want to repeat the experience.

Thorns grow in pairs

Hole through which ants enter thorn

Dried acacia twig

Gall

Ant

Barbs along edge of leaf

Long, sharp spines

Small, fleshy leaves

This nettle sting has been magnified many times to show the sharp tip

ANTS ON GUARD
Some acacia trees rely on ants to keep away browsing animals. In return for food and lodging the ants ferociously attack any animal which tries to feed on the tree's leaves. The ants eat the sweet-tasting pith of the thorns and make them hollow. They also feed from a row of nectaries at the base of each leaf. The bullhorn acacia even produces little knobs of protein and fat at the tip of each leaflet, which insures that the ants protect the whole leaf.

CHEMICAL WARFARE
The stings of the nettle are like hypodermic needles. The walls of the sting cell are covered with a glass-like substance called silica (p. 7). When an animal brushes past the nettle, the stings puncture its skin and release a cocktail of chemicals which causes a painful irritation. On future encounters animals remember the sting and avoid the nettle.

RUNNING INTO TROUBLE
Screw pines are tropical plants that have tough, sword-shaped leaves. These have rows of vicious barbs, not only along their edges, but also along their midribs. The barbs point away from the plant, so any animal trying to get near it runs the risk of being impaled, as it pushes forward.

Octopus tree

Barbs along midrib

Stinging nettle

PROTECTED LEAVES
Plants that live in hot, dry climates need to defend themselves because their leaves are a tempting source of food and water for animals. Many of them, such as cacti, do this with spines (pp. 52-53). This plant from Madagascar has spines that are longer than its leaves, making it very hard for large animals to reach them.

Leaf of screw pine

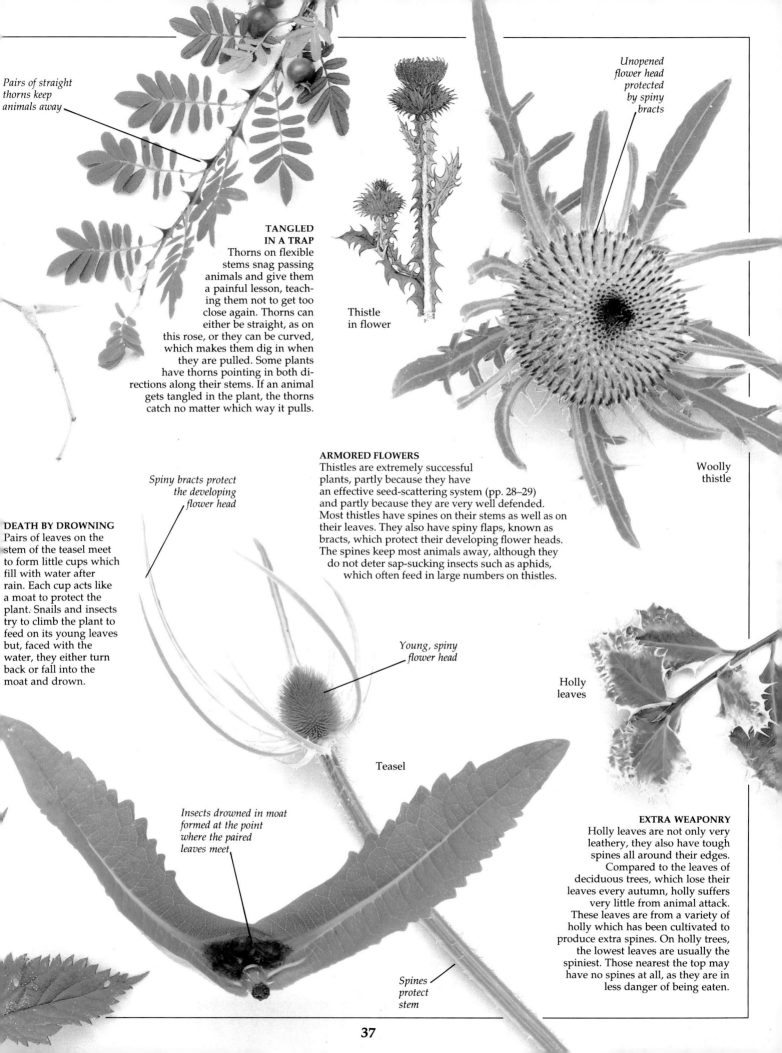

Pairs of straight thorns keep animals away

TANGLED IN A TRAP
Thorns on flexible stems snag passing animals and give them a painful lesson, teaching them not to get too close again. Thorns can either be straight, as on this rose, or they can be curved, which makes them dig in when they are pulled. Some plants have thorns pointing in both directions along their stems. If an animal gets tangled in the plant, the thorns catch no matter which way it pulls.

Thistle in flower

Unopened flower head protected by spiny bracts

Woolly thistle

ARMORED FLOWERS
Thistles are extremely successful plants, partly because they have an effective seed-scattering system (pp. 28–29) and partly because they are very well defended. Most thistles have spines on their stems as well as on their leaves. They also have spiny flaps, known as bracts, which protect their developing flower heads. The spines keep most animals away, although they do not deter sap-sucking insects such as aphids, which often feed in large numbers on thistles.

Spiny bracts protect the developing flower head

DEATH BY DROWNING
Pairs of leaves on the stem of the teasel meet to form little cups which fill with water after rain. Each cup acts like a moat to protect the plant. Snails and insects try to climb the plant to feed on its young leaves but, faced with the water, they either turn back or fall into the moat and drown.

Young, spiny flower head

Holly leaves

Teasel

Insects drowned in moat formed at the point where the paired leaves meet

EXTRA WEAPONRY
Holly leaves are not only very leathery, they also have tough spines all around their edges. Compared to the leaves of deciduous trees, which lose their leaves every autumn, holly suffers very little from animal attack. These leaves are from a variety of holly which has been cultivated to produce extra spines. On holly trees, the lowest leaves are usually the spiniest. Those nearest the top may have no spines at all, as they are in less danger of being eaten.

Spines protect stem

Creepers and climbers

WHEREVER THERE IS MOISTURE AND WARMTH, plants struggle against each other for light. The tallest plant usually gets the greatest share, but it also has to spend the most energy in growing a strong stem, or a tree trunk, to hold up its leaves. But there are some plants - epiphytes (pp. 46-47) and climbers - which take a shortcut to the top. They take advantage of other plants and even buildings to get a place in the light with much less effort. Epiphytes may grow on the trunks or upper branches of trees and are lifted up with them as they grow. These plants do not have roots on the ground and are able to absorb all the water they need from the air and rainwater. Climbers need supports. Some twine themselves around a plant; others put out touch-sensitive feelers, or tendrils, which curl around the support when they come into contact with it. A third group of climbers raise themselves by means of stiff side branches, prickles, roots, or hairs.

GROWING IN A SPIRAL
Plants which grow in a spiral twist in a set direction. Scarlet runner plants always twist in a clockwise direction, a detail noticed by the artist who made this 16th-century woodcut of a bean plant climbing up a stick.

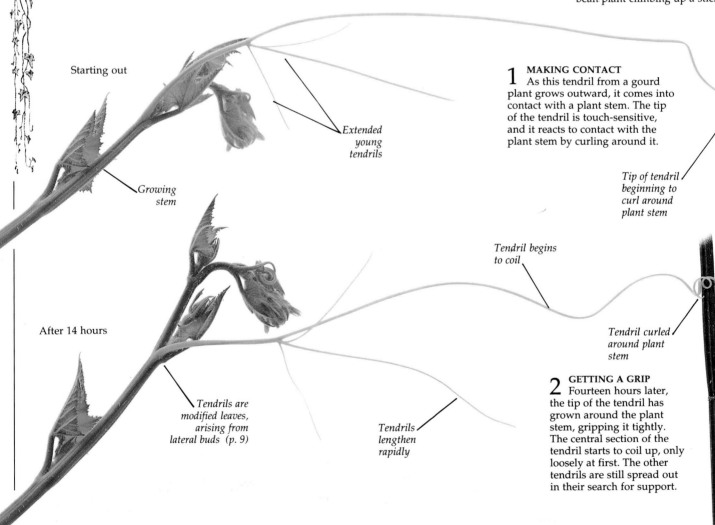

Starting out

Extended
young
tendrils

Growing
stem

After 14 hours

Tendrils are
modified leaves,
arising from
lateral buds (p. 9)

Tendrils
lengthen
rapidly

1 MAKING CONTACT
As this tendril from a gourd plant grows outward, it comes into contact with a plant stem. The tip of the tendril is touch-sensitive, and it reacts to contact with the plant stem by curling around it.

Tip of tendril
beginning to
curl around
plant stem

Tendril begins
to coil

Tendril curled
around plant
stem

2 GETTING A GRIP
Fourteen hours later, the tip of the tendril has grown around the plant stem, gripping it tightly. The central section of the tendril starts to coil up, only loosely at first. The other tendrils are still spread out in their search for support.

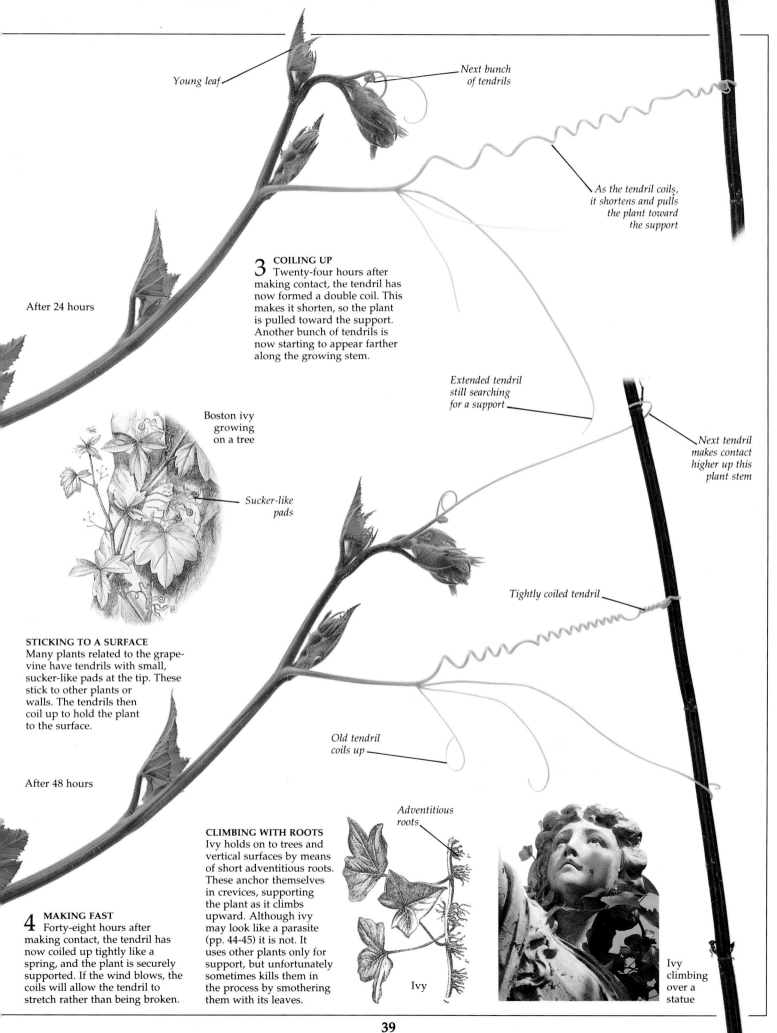

Young leaf

Next bunch of tendrils

As the tendril coils, it shortens and pulls the plant toward the support

3 COILING UP
Twenty-four hours after making contact, the tendril has now formed a double coil. This makes it shorten, so the plant is pulled toward the support. Another bunch of tendrils is now starting to appear farther along the growing stem.

After 24 hours

Boston ivy growing on a tree

Extended tendril still searching for a support

Next tendril makes contact higher up this plant stem

Sucker-like pads

Tightly coiled tendril

STICKING TO A SURFACE
Many plants related to the grape-vine have tendrils with small, sucker-like pads at the tip. These stick to other plants or walls. The tendrils then coil up to hold the plant to the surface.

Old tendril coils up

After 48 hours

Adventitious roots

CLIMBING WITH ROOTS
Ivy holds on to trees and vertical surfaces by means of short adventitious roots. These anchor themselves in crevices, supporting the plant as it climbs upward. Although ivy may look like a parasite (pp. 44-45) it is not. It uses other plants only for support, but unfortunately sometimes kills them in the process by smothering them with its leaves.

4 MAKING FAST
Forty-eight hours after making contact, the tendril has now coiled up tightly like a spring, and the plant is securely supported. If the wind blows, the coils will allow the tendril to stretch rather than being broken.

Ivy

Ivy climbing over a statue

Meat eaters

ALTHOUGH MAN-EATING PLANTS belong to the world of fiction, there are many plants that eat insects and other small animals. These meat-eating or carnivorous plants fall into two groups. Some species, such as the Venus flytrap (pp. 42-43), have active traps with moving parts that catch their prey. Other species have inactive traps with no moving parts. They simply attract their victims with a scent like that of food, and then catch them on a sticky surface or drown them in a pool of fluid. The victims of carnivorous plants are mostly insects. Once an insect has been caught, it is slowly dissolved by the plant's digestive fluids. After many days, all that is left is the insect's exoskeleton - the hard outer casing of the body. The rest of the insect has been absorbed by the plant. Carnivorous plants can make food from sunlight like ordinary plants. The insects they catch are simply used as a dietary supplement - they are the plants' equivalent of vitamin tablets. Many plants need this extra source of food because they grow in waterlogged ground, where the soil doesn't have many nitrates and other essential nutrients.

SPECIALIZED LEAVES
All the animal traps shown on these two pages are modified leaves. The leaves of the Portuguese sundew are so sticky that they used to be hung up indoors to catch flies.

Flower of Cape sundew

FATAL ATTRACTION
This colorful nepenthes pitcher lures passing insects.

Lid keeps out rain

Rim

THE STICKY SUNDEWS
The leaves of sundews are covered in hairs that produce droplets of sticky "glue." When an insect lands on one of the leaves, it sticks to the hairs, which then fold over and trap it.

Magnification of a fly trapped by hairs on sundew leaf

Cape sundew

Water flea trapped by a bladderwort

UNDERWATER TRAPS
Bladderworts are water plants that develop traps, in the form of tiny bladders, on their feathery leaves. If a small water animal swims past, the bubble-like bladder snaps open, and the animal is sucked inside.

LYING IN WAIT
Butterworts have circles of flat, sticky leaves. These plants may not look very threatening, but when an insect lands on a leaf, it becomes glued to the surface and eventually dies. The edges of the leaf very gradually curl inward, and the insect is digested. There are about 50 species of butterwort, most of which grow in marshy places.

Leaf covered with short, sticky hairs

Butterwort

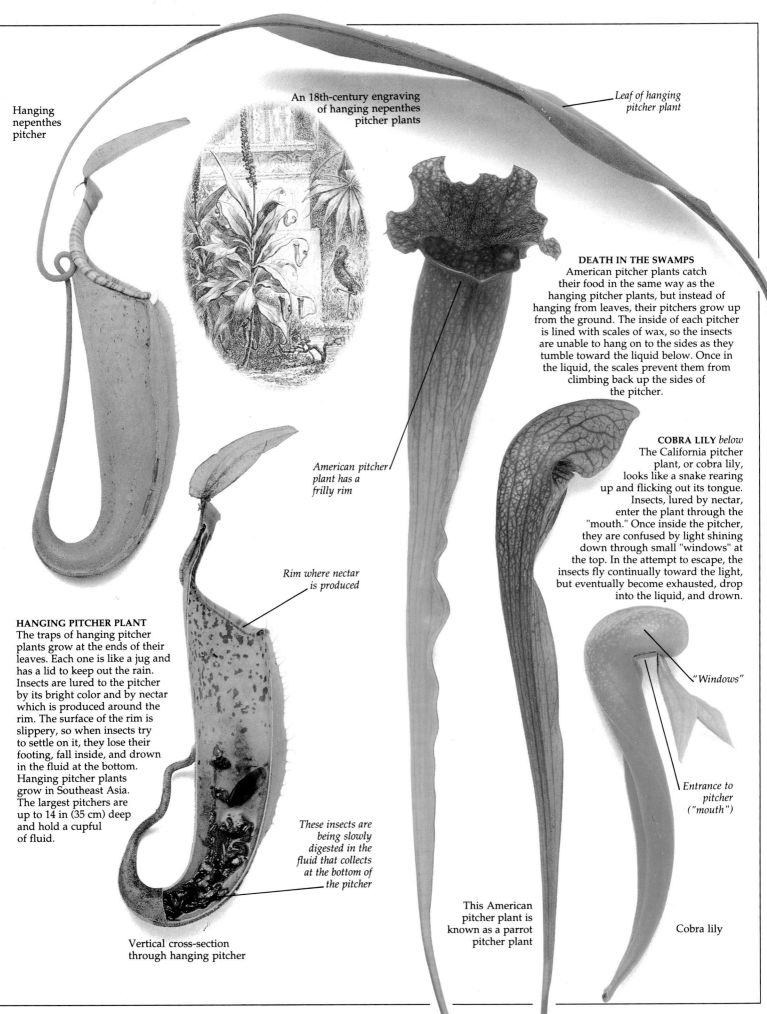

Hanging
nepenthes
pitcher

An 18th-century engraving
of hanging nepenthes
pitcher plants

*Leaf of hanging
pitcher plant*

DEATH IN THE SWAMPS
American pitcher plants catch
their food in the same way as the
hanging pitcher plants, but instead of
hanging from leaves, their pitchers grow up
from the ground. The inside of each pitcher
is lined with scales of wax, so the insects
are unable to hang on to the sides as they
tumble toward the liquid below. Once in
the liquid, the scales prevent them from
climbing back up the sides of
the pitcher.

COBRA LILY *below*
The California pitcher
plant, or cobra lily,
looks like a snake rearing
up and flicking out its tongue.
Insects, lured by nectar,
enter the plant through the
"mouth." Once inside the pitcher,
they are confused by light shining
down through small "windows" at
the top. In the attempt to escape, the
insects fly continually toward the light,
but eventually become exhausted, drop
into the liquid, and drown.

*American pitcher
plant has a
frilly rim*

*Rim where nectar
is produced*

HANGING PITCHER PLANT
The traps of hanging pitcher
plants grow at the ends of their
leaves. Each one is like a jug and
has a lid to keep out the rain.
Insects are lured to the pitcher
by its bright color and by nectar
which is produced around the
rim. The surface of the rim is
slippery, so when insects try
to settle on it, they lose their
footing, fall inside, and drown
in the fluid at the bottom.
Hanging pitcher plants
grow in Southeast Asia.
The largest pitchers are
up to 14 in (35 cm) deep
and hold a cupful
of fluid.

"Windows"

*Entrance to
pitcher
("mouth")*

*These insects are
being slowly
digested in the
fluid that collects
at the bottom of
the pitcher*

Vertical cross-section
through hanging pitcher

This American
pitcher plant is
known as a parrot
pitcher plant

Cobra lily

Caught in a trap

To AN UNWARY INSECT, the unusual leaf tips of the Venus flytrap appear most inviting. Not only is the insect attracted by what looks like a safe landing place, it is also tempted by the promise of food in the form of nectar. But it is all a trick. As soon as the insect settles, the leaf tips spring to life with lightning speed. Within a second, the hapless insect finds itself trapped as the two halves of the leaf snap shut. There is a second, slower phase of closing after the plant has tested what it has caught using sensory glands on the surface of its lobes. If the prey contains protein, the trap closes fully, and digestion begins. The traps of the Venus flytrap are formed by two kidney-shaped lobes at the tip of the leaf, with a hinge formed by the midrib. The entire leaf is green and therefore able to photosynthesize (pp. 14-15). Large bristles on the upper surface of the trap work like triggers with a clever device. If just one bristle is touched, by a raindrop for example, the trap stays open. But if two or more bristles are touched one after the other, it quickly shuts to catch its victim.

A MOST HORRIBLE TORTURE
Insects were not the only ones to be condemned to a frightful and lingering death, as this rather gruesome engraving shows.

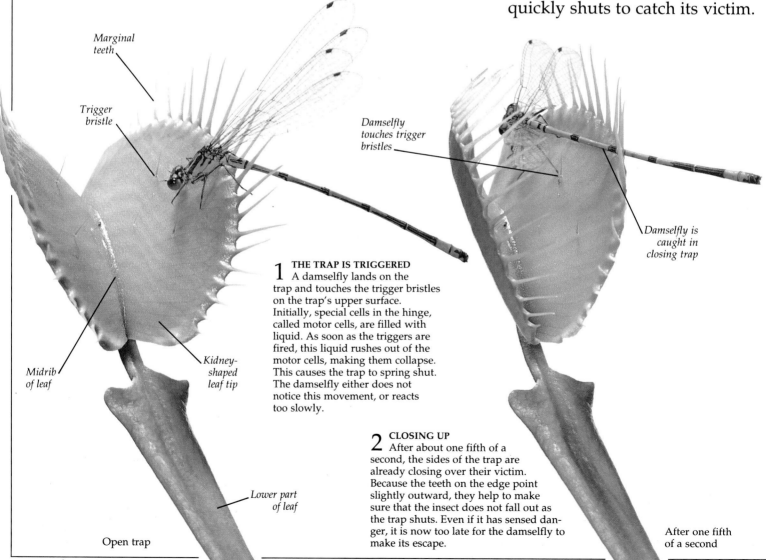

Marginal teeth

Trigger bristle

Midrib of leaf

Kidney-shaped leaf tip

Lower part of leaf

Open trap

Damselfly touches trigger bristles

Damselfly is caught in closing trap

1 THE TRAP IS TRIGGERED
A damselfly lands on the trap and touches the trigger bristles on the trap's upper surface. Initially, special cells in the hinge, called motor cells, are filled with liquid. As soon as the triggers are fired, this liquid rushes out of the motor cells, making them collapse. This causes the trap to spring shut. The damselfly either does not notice this movement, or reacts too slowly.

2 CLOSING UP
After about one fifth of a second, the sides of the trap are already closing over their victim. Because the teeth on the edge point slightly outward, they help to make sure that the insect does not fall out as the trap shuts. Even if it has sensed danger, it is now too late for the damselfly to make its escape.

After one fifth of a second

An early
19th-century
painting of
the Venus
flytrap by
Redoute, who
painted the
plants kept by
the Empress
Josephine at
Malmaison
(p. 61)

*Flower
stem*

*Open
trap*

GROWING A FLYTRAP
The first living specimen of
the Venus flytrap arrived in
England from America in the
mid-18th century. Never
before had such an unusual
and spectacular plant been
seen live in Europe, and it
aroused great curiosity
among botanists. Today
Venus flytraps can be grown
as potted plants. Because
they come from waterlogged
bogs with slightly acid soil,
they must never be allowed
to dry out and are best
planted in peat. It is
important to water them
with distilled water, because
tap water often contains
dissolved minerals that
will reduce the plant's
chances of survival.
Venus flytraps do produce
clusters of white flowers,
but this does not often
happen with indoor
specimens, especially if
they are frequently fed
with insects.

A WATERY HABITAT
Venus flytraps come from the bogs
of North Carolina. Each plant
grows from a small rhizome and
produces several traps. Each trap
can catch about three insects before
it withers.

FLOATING TRAPS
This waterwheel plant is a
small water plant that
belongs to the same family
of plants as the Venus
flytrap and the sundews. Its
leaves end in small traps
that catch tiny water
animals. They can close in
one fiftieth of a second.

*Marginal
teeth
closing
around
insect*

*Teeth on
edge form a
cage around
the damselfly*

Trap almost closed

3 COMING TOGETHER
After two fifths of a second,
the teeth have almost met. They
are arranged alternately, so that
they do not crash into each other as
the trap closes. Meanwhile, inside
the trap, the trigger bristles fold
back. This insures that they are not
damaged and will be able to work
again when the trap reopens.

4 ALL EXITS SEALED
When the trap shuts, its sides
remain at a slight angle to each
other. At this stage very small insects
can climb out between the teeth, but
the damselfly is too big and is securely
held in. The trap would be wasted on
small insects, as it can only digest two
or three insects before it becomes
ineffective. After 30 minutes the sides
of the trap will close fully and the
plant will begin to digest its prisoner.

5 DIGESTION
Special glands
inside the trap secrete
acid and substances
called enzymes which
will slowly digest all
the soft parts of the
insect's body. These
glands later absorb the
digested insect. It will
take about two weeks for
the damselfly to be fully
digested, and for the trap
to be ready for another
meal. When the trap re-
opens, the insect's hard
exoskeleton, which includes
the wings, will blow away.

After two fifths
of a second

Parasitic plants

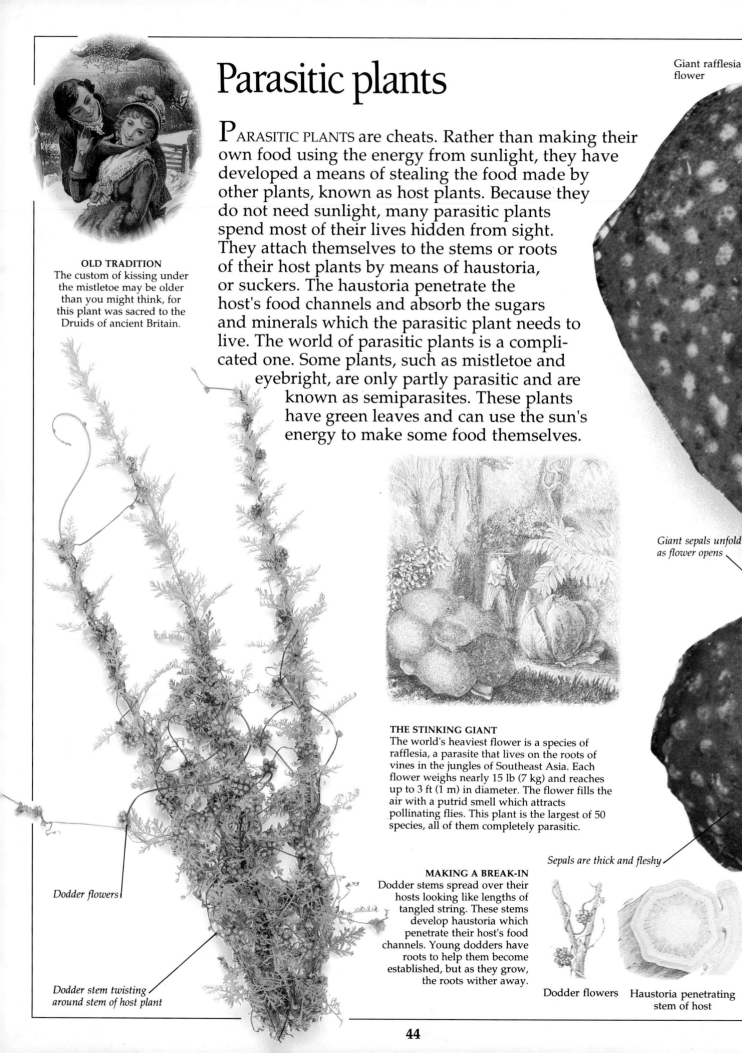

Giant rafflesia flower

PARASITIC PLANTS are cheats. Rather than making their own food using the energy from sunlight, they have developed a means of stealing the food made by other plants, known as host plants. Because they do not need sunlight, many parasitic plants spend most of their lives hidden from sight. They attach themselves to the stems or roots of their host plants by means of haustoria, or suckers. The haustoria penetrate the host's food channels and absorb the sugars and minerals which the parasitic plant needs to live. The world of parasitic plants is a complicated one. Some plants, such as mistletoe and eyebright, are only partly parasitic and are known as semiparasites. These plants have green leaves and can use the sun's energy to make some food themselves.

OLD TRADITION
The custom of kissing under the mistletoe may be older than you might think, for this plant was sacred to the Druids of ancient Britain.

Giant sepals unfold as flower opens

THE STINKING GIANT
The world's heaviest flower is a species of rafflesia, a parasite that lives on the roots of vines in the jungles of Southeast Asia. Each flower weighs nearly 15 lb (7 kg) and reaches up to 3 ft (1 m) in diameter. The flower fills the air with a putrid smell which attracts pollinating flies. This plant is the largest of 50 species, all of them completely parasitic.

Sepals are thick and fleshy

MAKING A BREAK-IN
Dodder stems spread over their hosts looking like lengths of tangled string. These stems develop haustoria which penetrate their host's food channels. Young dodders have roots to help them become established, but as they grow, the roots wither away.

Dodder flowers

Dodder stem twisting around stem of host plant

Dodder flowers   Haustoria penetrating stem of host

Plant passengers

NOT ALL PLANTS that live on others are parasites (pp. 44-45). In fact, many more of them are simply passengers that grow on larger plants, such as trees, without causing them any harm. Such plants are described as "epiphytic," and many of them can get all the water they need simply by absorbing it from the air or by collecting it in structures formed for the purpose. They collect minerals by removing them from trickling rainwater and plant debris. Being an epiphyte gives a small plant a chance to absorb a lot of light without the need of tall stems. So successful is this way of life that few trees are without their passengers. In cool parts of the world, epiphytes are usually small, simple plants, such as algae, lichens, and mosses. But in moist regions close to the equator, they are much larger. As well as the plants that spend their entire lives up in the trees, there are others that start or end their lives in this way. Some creeping plants, known as stranglers, germinate on trees and then become rooted in the soil. Others climb up onto plants but then their roots wither away, leaving them perched high up near the light.

These large, woody climbers, known as lianas, grow in tropical rain forests

Leaves have a special coating to reduce water loss

In the forests of Sri Lanka, epiphytic orchids grow on the trees

THE BROMELIAD'S PRIVATE POND
The bromeliads are a family of plants which includes the pineapple. Many of them grow on other plants. Instead of collecting water with long, aerial roots like orchids, they channel rainwater into a central reservoir (right) with their stiff, spiky leaves. Hairs on the leaves then absorb the water so the plant can use it. A big bromeliad holds over 1 gallon (5 liters) of water, and provides a home for water animals such as tree-frog tadpoles.

A species of
moth orchid

EPIPHYTIC ORCHIDS
There are about 18,000 species of orchid in the world. Many tropical orchids live by perching on other plants. Orchid seeds are tiny, and a single plant may produce a million of them. The wind blows the seeds of epiphytic species onto the bark of trees, where they can germinate. Each of these perching orchids has three types of aerial root, for clinging to the host, for absorbing minerals, and for taking water from the atmosphere. Some epiphytic orchids store water and food reserves in swollen stems called pseudobulbs.

Flowers produce wind-scattered seeds

Thick, trailing aerial roots collect moisture as well as minerals from trickling rainwater

Liana stems make a natural rope

NATURAL ROPES
Lianas are climbing plants with flexible woody stems. Sometimes they twine around each other for mutual support. If the original support dies and decays, the lianas are left suspended from the forest canopy. Other plants, called stranglers, start life above ground and then grow roots downward. Their roots form a mesh around the trunks of trees and eventually kill the support.

Tarzan used lianas to swing from tree to tree across the jungle

Adapting to water

THE FIRST PLANTS ON EARTH evolved in water. Today water still teems with microscopic plants that have changed little from those distant ancestors. But aquatic flowering plants have a different history. Their ancestors originally left water and evolved on land, but as time went by they returned to a watery habitat. Only a few flowering plants, such as the eelgrasses, live in the sea. Far more plant species live in freshwater ponds, lakes, and rivers. Most of them are rooted to the bottom, but some have no roots and receive all the nutrients they need from the water instead of the soil. Some water plants are not often noticed because they spend all their lives underwater. Species like the water lily are easier to spot because their leaves float on the surface. Plants such as reeds and rushes form a group known as emergent plants. They grow up out of the water and often form thick beds at the water's edge.

HISTORIC HIDEOUT
The pharaoh's daughter discovers Moses hidden in the bulrushes at the water's edge.

Glossy yellow flowers

LEAVING THE WATER
The greater spearwort is an example of an emergent water plant. It starts its annual cycle of growth underwater but quickly reaches the surface. The flowers bloom about 2 ft (60 cm) above the water, where they attract pollinating insects.

Greater spearwort

Spear-shaped leaves

UNDERWATER LEAVES
Fanwort has finely divided underwater leaves which are not damaged by the current.

Fanwort

19th-century engraving of papyrus growing by the Nile in Egypt

FLOATING ON THE SURFACE
When young, the leaves of water lilies are rolled up underwater like short tubes. In spring, the leaves reach the surface, where they open out and lie flat to form pads. In some ponds and lakes, water lilies and other plants with floating leaves can completely cover the water's surface, robbing submerged plants of the light they need to survive. The leaves are tough and leathery so water easily runs off their surface.

Tough, waxy surface repels water

Flexible stalks attach leaves to the roots, which are anchored in the muddy bottom

A PLANT FOR PAPER
Papyrus is a giant reed that grows up to 10 ft (3 m) high. The Ancient Egyptians discovered that the pith in the middle of its stems could be used to make a material for writing on – the very first paper.

AMAZONIAN GIANT
The floating leaves of the Amazonian water lily can reach a diameter of more than 6 ft (2 m).

Surviving above the snowline

THE HIGHER THE ALTITUDE at which a plant grows, the colder the temperatures it has to endure. Very low temperatures create specific problems for plant life. Thin mountain air holds little heat, and on exposed mountainsides, high winds create a chill factor which makes the cold even more penetrating. In addition, low rainfall and thin, frozen soils mean that water is scarce. However, many plants manage to survive despite the harsh conditions. In the Himalayas, flowering plants have been found at over 20,000 ft (6,000 m), sheltering in hollows in the frost-shattered rock. These plants, known as alpine plants, are generally small and compact so they can survive on the high mountain peaks or in the frozen polar regions. Alpine plants often grow in dense cushions or flattened mats, giving them protection against the cold, drying wind. Upright, spreading branches would quickly be battered by the wind, and large leaves would lose valuable heat and water.

An unsteady perch for a determined alpine plant collector

Mountain avens

Mountain kidney vetch

QUICK WORK
When spring comes, the mountain slopes burst into color as alpine plants begin to flower. In high mountain areas where the summers are short, these plants have to flower and produce seeds quickly before winter comes around again.

BUILT IN SUNSCREENS
This mountain kidney vetch grows high in the Alps and has leaves covered in hairs. Like those of the silversword, the hairs protect the leaves from sun damage, reduce water loss, and act as insulation.

HAIRY LEAVES
Mountain avens are plants that grow on high ground, from the Alps to the Arctic. Fine hairs on the undersides of their leaves keep them from losing too much water and act as insulation.

RADIATION HAZARD
The sunlight that falls on high mountaintops in the tropics is more intense than anywhere else on Earth. The silversword grows in Hawaii at altitudes of up to 13,000 ft (4,000 m). Its leaves are covered with fine white hairs which protect the plant from much of the sun's dangerous ultraviolet radiation.

PLANT CUSHIONS
This dwarf hebe from New Zealand is an evergreen plant with small tough leaves that can withstand sharp frost. It grows in dense cushions which trap heat, prevent wind damage, and reduce water loss. These cushions are covered in white flowers every spring.

Dwarf hebe

Garland
flower

Alpine
moltkia

FLAT AGAINST THE GROUND
Mazus reptans

Many alpine plants spread over the ground in the form of flat mats, keeping out of the path of icy winds. This "prostrate" or mat-forming plant, *Mazus reptans*, is from the Himalayas.

A MINIATURE SHRUB
This alpine daphne, or garland flower, is a shrub in miniature. Larger daphnes grow at lower levels.

SMALL LEAVES
Moltkias are members of the forget-me-not family. Unlike many of their lowland relatives, alpine moltkias have small leaves which are better able to withstand high winds.

MOUNDS OF COLOR
Like many alpine plants, this beautiful phlox from North America has brilliantly colored flowers. They stand out against the rocky slopes and attract pollinating insects.

Hoary rockrose

Alpine
phlox

DUAL PROTECTION
Mountain rockroses are protected from the weather in two ways. The bushy plants are able to stand up to strong wind better than those with taller, more rigid stems, and their leaves and stems are covered with fine hairs which act as insulation at night.

TWO WAYS TO SPREAD
This species of storksbill lives in the high Pyrenees. It spreads both by seeds and by its creeping root system (p. 32).

MOUNTAIN DWARF
Many mountain plants which survive at great heights, like this St.-John's-wort, are much smaller than their lowland relatives.

St.-John's-
wort

Storksbill

Living without water

No PLANT CAN LIVE entirely without water, but in very dry regions, where water is scarce, some plants, called succulents, are able to survive for a number of years between rainstorms. In the world's driest places, rain often comes in irregular but heavy bursts, so the plants that live there have evolved ways of collecting as much water as possible during downpours. The water is then stored in preparation for the next drought. Many succulents have very long roots, most of which grow near the surface, so that when it rains, they can collect water from a wide area. Once the water is inside the plant, it is kept there by a number of special adaptations. Plants normally lose water from stomata, tiny pores in the leaf surface. The plant can control these pores and keeps them closed if it begins to lose too much water. Many succulents open the pores only at night, when the air is cool and less water can evaporate. Some of these plants have got around the problem of water loss by losing their leaves altogether.

Mammillaria elongata

Ferocactus

Echinocereus

Fake flowers stuck on by a clever florist to enhance the plant's appearance

THE CACTUS FAMILY
Almost all true cacti come from the Americas. Because they live in very dry places, they have had to evolve strange shapes to be able to survive. Most cacti have very thick stems and thick groups of spines instead of normal leaves. These spines may protect the plant from heat and cold as well as from attack by animals. Many cacti have ridges down their stems to allow them to expand and store water when it rains.

Cross-section of square stem

Row of spines

Clusters of spines

Big-toothed euphorbia

SIMILAR SHAPES FOR SIMILAR LIFESTYLES
Not all the spiny plants that live in dry places are cacti. The cactus-like plant on the far left is actually a spurge, a plant quite unrelated to the two cacti to its right. Like the cacti, it has lost its leaves and developed a tough, water-holding stem. This is a typical example of "convergent evolution," in which plants or animals in similar environments evolve in similar ways.

Prickly pear cactus

Cleistocactus

Cross-section of round stem

THE GIANT SAGUARO
The saguaro is one of the world's tallest cacti. A 250-year-old plant can be 50 ft (15 m) high and can weigh 6 tons.

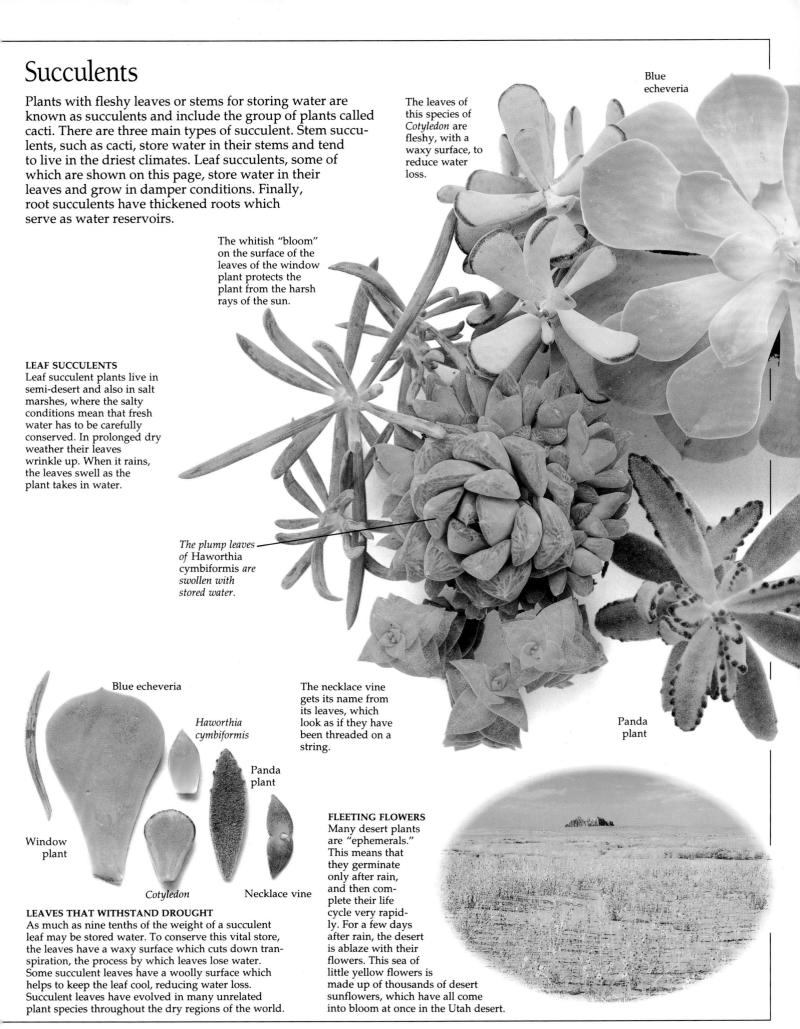

Succulents

Plants with fleshy leaves or stems for storing water are known as succulents and include the group of plants called cacti. There are three main types of succulent. Stem succulents, such as cacti, store water in their stems and tend to live in the driest climates. Leaf succulents, some of which are shown on this page, store water in their leaves and grow in damper conditions. Finally, root succulents have thickened roots which serve as water reservoirs.

The leaves of this species of *Cotyledon* are fleshy, with a waxy surface, to reduce water loss.

Blue echeveria

The whitish "bloom" on the surface of the leaves of the window plant protects the plant from the harsh rays of the sun.

LEAF SUCCULENTS
Leaf succulent plants live in semi-desert and also in salt marshes, where the salty conditions mean that fresh water has to be carefully conserved. In prolonged dry weather their leaves wrinkle up. When it rains, the leaves swell as the plant takes in water.

The plump leaves of Haworthia cymbiformis *are swollen with stored water.*

Blue echeveria

Haworthia cymbiformis

The necklace vine gets its name from its leaves, which look as if they have been threaded on a string.

Panda plant

Window plant

Panda plant

Cotyledon

Necklace vine

FLEETING FLOWERS
Many desert plants are "ephemerals." This means that they germinate only after rain, and then complete their life cycle very rapidly. For a few days after rain, the desert is ablaze with their flowers. This sea of little yellow flowers is made up of thousands of desert sunflowers, which have all come into bloom at once in the Utah desert.

LEAVES THAT WITHSTAND DROUGHT
As much as nine tenths of the weight of a succulent leaf may be stored water. To conserve this vital store, the leaves have a waxy surface which cuts down transpiration, the process by which leaves lose water. Some succulent leaves have a woolly surface which helps to keep the leaf cool, reducing water loss. Succulent leaves have evolved in many unrelated plant species throughout the dry regions of the world.

Food from plants

PLANTS HAVE BEEN CULTIVATED as food crops for thousands of years. The earliest humans lived in nomadic groups, roaming the countryside in search of food. Eventually these peoples settled down, and instead of collecting plant foods from the wild they began to cultivate them. When the time came to gather seeds to produce crops for the following year, they tended to take seeds from the healthiest plants. As they did this year after year, they began to produce better crop plants. Later, more deliberate efforts were made to improve crops by selecting and cultivating the strongest plants, and this process is continuing today. As farming settlements were established independently in different parts of the world, so different crops were cultivated in each place. This meant that when early travelers first visited distant continents, they found many new and exciting foods to bring home. The crops we eat today come from many different parts of the world.

MARKET IN PERU
Potatoes originated in the high Andes of South America. Many varieties of potato are still grown there, as this market scene shows.

KEPT IN THE DARK
If allowed to grow in the light, chicory has a bitter taste. To reduce this bitterness, the plant is cut back to the ground and then allowed to regrow with almost no light. The pale, "blanched" leaves of the new chicory shoot are far less bitter. If cultivated chicory were grown entirely in the light, the plant would look very similar to its ancestor.

Primitive form of corn plant and cob

Blanched shoot of cultivated chicory

Modern corncob

Wild chicory

PRIMITIVE CORN
Corn is a cereal; like wheat and rice it is a member of the grass family. It was first cultivated in Central America, and some primitive forms of corn can still be found growing there. As a result of selective breeding, the size and shape of the modern corncob have been increased.

Fruits of a wild tomato, from Mexico

Flowers of wild tomato; flowers of cultivated tomato are very similar.

Wild cabbage has dark green, leathery leaves

LEAVING THE PAST BEHIND
The wild cabbage grows near the sea. It has leathery leaves, loosely arranged on a branched stem. Years of breeding have got rid of the plant's bitter taste and made its leaves more juicy. The shape of the plant has also changed so that, in most cultivated cabbages, the leaves are packed tightly together. In the "red" varieties of cabbage, certain natural pigments have been built up as a result of selective breeding.

Beefsteak tomato

Cultivated tomatoes have become much bigger through breeding.

BIGGER - AND BETTER?
The tomato's wild ancestor is a red berry the size of a small grape. It is much sweeter than the modern tomato, and more strongly flavored.

GROWING IN WATER
Rice, which was cultivated in the Far East at least 5,000 years ago, forms the staple cereal diet of over one half of the world's population. It usually grows in fields of standing water, known as paddies.

Flower head of wild carrot

Working in the paddies

Modern cabbage

Wild carrot root

Cultivated carrot

Modern red cabbage

EDIBLE ROOTS
The wild carrot is found all over Europe and through much of Asia, but its roots are white or only slightly colored. Only in Afghanistan is there a variety of wild carrot with orange roots. The carrot was probably first cultivated in that region and then introduced to other parts of the world.

CARROTS AND CABBAGES
This detail from a 16th-century painting by the Dutch artist Lucas Van Valkenborch proves that even 400 years ago there was a wide variety of vegetables available.

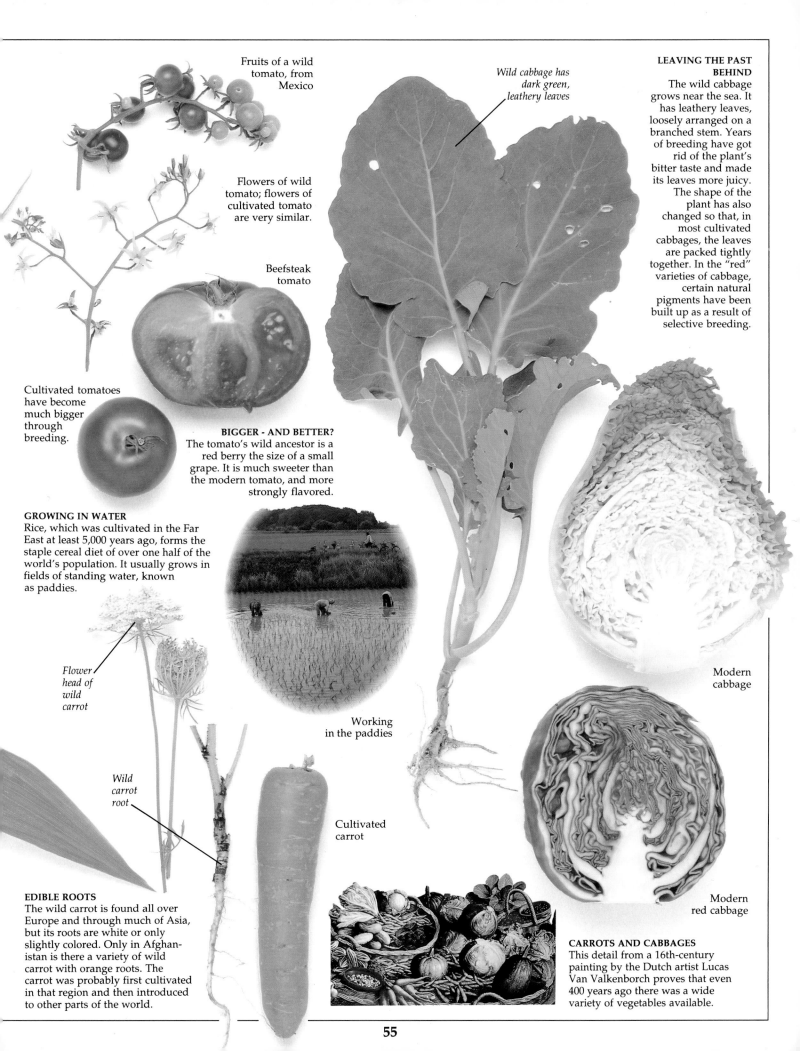

The story of wheat

WHEAT HAS BEEN CULTIVATED by humans as a valuable source of food for at least 9,000 years. Grains of wheat have been found preserved in ancient Egyptian tombs, and it is known that it was the chief cereal of the ancient Greeks and Romans. The cultivation of wheat originated in the region known as the Fertile Crescent, which includes part of Israel, Turkey, Iraq, and Iran. Once a rich farming area, today much of it is desert. Wheat is now grown in most parts of the world and the quality has improved greatly. The early, primitive species, such as einkorn and emmer, had long thin stalks which were easily broken in bad weather. The small grains meant that a large number of plants only produced a relatively low yield of grain. Today, as a result of extensive breeding programs, better varieties have been found which have higher yields, resist drought, and withstand disease.

FOOD FOR THE MASSES
People have grown cereals for food for thousands of years, as this picture from the 11th century shows.

CUTTING THE CORN
Wild grasses drop their ripe seeds. The first farmers selected plants that held on to the seeds, so that the grain could be harvested.

Grains of wild einkorn

Grains of emmer

WILD EINKORN
This wild grass is probably one of the ancestors of all cultivated wheats. It has long, thin stalks and small heads and grains.

EINKORN
This early wheat species is still grown in parts of Turkey for animal feed. Its grains are small and difficult to thresh.

WILD WHEAT
This wild grass is the ancestor of emmer, another primitive wheat. The heads and grains are larger than those of einkorn.

EMMER
Emmer was the chief cereal in ancient Greek and Roman times. It is one of the ancestors of modern cultivated wheats.

The long, spiky bristles attached to scales around each grain are called awns

Spelt grains

Today's wheat is much shorter than that of a century ago. Breeders have reduced the amount of stalk, so that the plant does not bend over; a curved stalk makes it difficult to harvest the grain. This is an important step forward for the major grain-producing countries of the world, where vast areas of wheat are grown.

SPELT
The great leap forward for wheats came when emmer crossed, or hybridized, with wild goat grass that was growing as a weed in wheat fields. The result was spelt wheat, which is still cultivated in parts of northwest Europe.

Brown bread baked with unbleached whole-wheat flour

Durum wheat

Pasta shells

DURUM WHEAT
Another large-grain wheat closely related to emmer is durum, or macaroni, wheat. It is grown widely today to provide the flour for pasta. It is not used for making bread because it has a low content of gluten - the substance that makes bread light and airy. Modern durum wheat has bigger grains as a result of intensive breeding.

Bread wheat

Uncooked whole-wheat flour

BREAD WHEAT
Bread wheat is also a hybrid between emmer and wild goat grass and is the most widely grown modern wheat. Its large grains have a high gluten content which makes bread dough elastic and enables light, airy bread to be made.

White bread, made from very finely ground flour that has been bleached

Potions and poisons

IN ANCIENT TIMES, plants were the main source of medicines. By trial and error, it was discovered that particular species could cure certain diseases. These plants were often grown in special gardens, and their details noted in plant reference books called herbals. Today many plants are still used in medicine. The chemicals they produce may be poisonous in large quantities, but small amounts can prove very useful in the treatment of some illnesses. The search for new medicines continues today, and every year pharmacologists examine thousands of plants from all over the world.

MANDRAKE
The mandrake root, once used in medicines, sometimes looks almost human. It was usually pulled up by a dog, because, according to an old superstition, the root would shriek as it came out of the ground. Any human who heard the noise would die.

Aloe vera

Cosmetic preparation made from aloe vera

Jojoba

COSMETIC EFFECT
Plants are often used in cosmetics for their pleasant smell or soothing oils. Two plants that are popular in today's cosmetics are jojoba and aloe vera. Both live in dry places and contain oils that help to keep skin soft.

OUT OF THE EAST
In China, ginseng has been prized for about 5,000 years. The powdered root has a stimulant effect and can aid recovery from illness. Ginseng is grown commercially and is now sold all over the world.

Red ginseng root from Korea

Opium poppies growing in Turkey

THE OPIUM POPPY
For thousands of years opium poppies have been grown as a source of drugs. Raw opium is the poppy's dried sap. It oozes out of the unripe seed head after it has been scarred with a knife. Opium is used in the manufacture of morphine, codeine, and heroin - drugs which can be deadly if misused.

Beans contain oil and poisonous ricin

Detail of a page from a 12th-century herbal

Castor-oil plant

A DEADLY DOSE
The oil from the beans of the castor-oil plant has been used to purify the system since the days of the ancient Egyptians. The beans also contain ricin, one of the most potent poisons known. Ricin is so powerful that, if eaten, just one bean is enough to kill an adult.

Leaves of
the dumb
cane

THE DUMB CANE
The name of this plant comes
from its poisonous sap. If
the sap is swallowed, it
makes the mouth
swell so much that
talking becomes
difficult.

DRINK OR DRUG?
The mescal cactus *Lophophora
williamsii* contains a substance
called mescaline which causes
hallucinations and is used in the
religious rituals of certain Mexican
Indian tribes. The Mexican drink
mescal is not derived from the
mescal cactus *Lophophora*,
but from another Mexican
plant, *Agave
tequilana*.

Mescal
cactus

The drink
mescal is made
from the plant
*Agave
tequilana*

DEADLY BERRIES
The drug atropine, which is used in
eye surgery and to treat stomach
complaints, is derived from
a very poisonous plant
called belladonna, or
deadly nightshade.

FROM COCA TO COCAINE
Many centuries ago, South
American Indians discovered
that chewing the leaves of the
coca plant dulled pain and
prevented tiredness. Coca
leaves contain the drug
cocaine. Although a
valuable anaesthetic,
cocaine can be
dangerously
addictive.

Coca leaves for sale

Coca leaves

Foxglove

This group in India at
the end of the 19th
century are relaxing
with a gin and tonic

Belladonna,
or deadly
nightshade

**HELP FOR
THE HEART**
The leaves of the
foxglove contain
digitalis, a sub-
stance used to treat
heart conditions. In
large doses, it
produces palpitations
and dizziness, but in
smaller doses, it helps
the heart to beat more
slowly and strongly.

A CURE FOR MALARIA
Quinine, which is used in the
treatment of malaria, is obtained
from the bark of South American
cinchona trees. Quinine is also used as
a bitter flavor in tonic water, a drink
which is commonly mixed with gin.

Cinchona
leaves

The plant collectors

MANY OF THE PLANTS that have become common in gardens all over the world are, in fact, very far from home. Most fuchsias, for example, come originally from South America, wisteria from China and Japan, many azaleas from the Himalayas, and tulips from western and central Asia. These are just some of the thousands of plants that have been carried across the world by plant collectors. Plant collecting had its heyday in the 19th and early 20th centuries, as intrepid botanists traveled farther and farther afield in search of unknown plants. Some plant collectors experienced great hardships on their voyages to distant places - being shot at, caught in earthquakes, and attacked by wild animals. But despite all such adversities, the lure of making new discoveries spurred them on to explore some of the world's most remote and dangerous places.

Scutellaria tournefortii is named after its discoverer, Joseph Pitton de Tournefort

ROYAL MISSION
Joseph Pitton de Tournefort (1656-1708) was a botanist who was sent to the eastern Mediterranean by the French king Louis XIV. He returned with the specimens and seeds of over a thousand plants, many of which became garden favorites.

A 19th-century plant collector with his collecting case, or vasculum

A 19th-century vasculum containing *Sarcococca hookerana*, a species of sweet box, one of many plants named by the Hookers

GOING EAST
The photograph above shows botanists on a plant-collecting expedition to China in the 1920s. This region of the world has been of great interest to botanists for many years, and expeditions made there today still discover new plant species. The photograph on the right shows a botanist on a modern plant-collecting expedition.

FATHER AND SON
William Hooker (1785-1865) and his son Joseph (1817-1911) were both passionately interested in plants. William Hooker became the first director of the Royal Botanic Gardens at Kew in England. Joseph is especially remembered for collecting many species of rhododendron in the Himalayas.

Leaves of sycamore

Tradescant father and son

GOING WEST
John Tradescant and his son, also named John, were English plantsmen. Tradescant the elder collected in Russia, and Tradescant the younger collected in America. The younger Tradescant imported trees into Europe. These included the tulip tree and the sycamore.

FIT FOR ROYALTY
Plant collecting is an ancient pursuit. This Egyptian mural shows the earliest recorded expedition, which took place in 1495 B.C. Collectors brought back frankincense trees for Queen Hatshepsut from the Horn of Africa.

Tradescantia - a border plant named after John Tradescant the elder

Beautifully preserved botanical reference books

THE EMPRESS COLLECTOR
Empress Josephine, the wife of Napoleon, created a unique garden at her house at Malmaison with roses brought from all around the world. At the time France was at war with Britain, but ships carrying the imperial roses were allowed safe passage.

Herbarium
specimen
sheet

Looking at plants

P LANT COLLECTIONS are of two kinds -
living plants and preserved specimens.
The preserved specimens are mostly
pressed and are kept in a herbarium,
where they can be examined by botanists.
Collections of living plants are equally important and sometimes insure that rare plant species
do not die out. Making your own collection of flowers
and pressing them is a good way to learn about plants.
However, you should not pick flowers that are growing
wild in the countryside, as this prevents them from producing seeds. Some wildflower species are very rare and
are protected by law; check with local authorities to find out
what they are. If you want to try to grow your own plants, you
can collect small amounts of seed or you can buy wildflower seeds,
produced by plants that have been raised in nurseries.
Growing your own plants gives you a
chance to study them without harming
plants in the wild.

Preserving
bottle

Box
containing
dried specimen

Plant press

HERB. HORT. REG. B

Na echinacea

Forest, Lincs

47818
HERB. HORT. BOT. REG. KEW.

Dendrobium (lindleyi) aggregatum Rd

Thailand   Menzies & July
                                     89

BOTANIST'S COLLECTING EQUIPMENT
Specimens being collected for a herbarium
are pressed and then mounted on a
herbarium sheet with a label saying
where and when they were found. The
herbarium sheet can then be
consulted by botanists wishing
to study the plants in detail.

Pruning
shears

Trowel

Sketchbook

Magnifying glass

LEARNING MORE ABOUT PLANTS
One of the best ways of finding out more about wildflowers is to draw or photograph them. If you draw them, you will notice many details about their structure, which will help you to identify the plant family. A magnifying glass can be useful for examining leaves and petals more closely. Collecting seeds and growing plants from them requires patience and care. Stored seeds should always be kept dry. Many seeds will germinate better if they are left in a refrigerator for a few weeks before planting. This cold period simulates the low winter temperatures they may experience in the wild. Large seeds, like those from sweet peas, germinate more quickly if they are first scratched, or "scarified," with sandpaper.

Scissors

Camera

Envelopes for collecting seed

PRESERVING SPECIMENS
Plants can be pressed with a simple screw press. The specimens are laid between two sheets of absorbent paper, which should be replaced with dry sheets every day or so. It can take a few weeks for specimens to dry out.

Plant press

Top for plant press

Screws for tightening plant press

Did you know?

AMASING FACTS

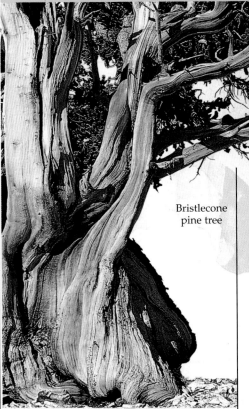

Bristlecone pine tree

The oldest seed known to botany comes from the North American Arctic lupine plant and is thought to be about 10,000 years old. The tendency of lupine seeds to be naturally preserved by the cold gave scientists the idea to place seeds in cold storage as stock for the future.

The oldest individual living plant is thought to be the bristlecone pine (*Pinus aristata*). One such plant has been dated at 4,900 years old, although a huge huon pine (*Dacrydium franklinii*) recently found in Tasmania may be older.

The orchid family has more species than any other flowering plant, with 25,000–30,000 species recognized, mostly in tropical regions. Orchids are found in every continent except for Antarctica and inhabit just about every type of environment except for extreme deserts and salt water.

Arctic lupine

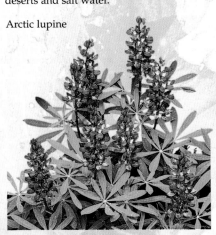

The fynbos, or evergreen bushland, of the Cape region in South Africa, contains one of the world's densest concentrations of plants within a small area. The east and north coasts around Cape Town are home to an amazing range of aloes, proteas, and ericas. There are an estimated 6,500 plant species in this tiny region—almost as many as on the entire continent of Europe.

Sphagnum moss, which is found in bogs and contributes to the formation of peat, can soak up more than 25 times its own dry weight in moisture.

Much less is known about small plants than large ones. Scientists estimate that they have identified 85–90 percent of flowering plants but only about 5 percent of the world's microscopic organisms.

The largest fruit is the pumpkin, which can weigh up to 1,130 lb (513 kg). Its close rival is the squash, which has been known to grow to 893 lb (405 kg).

The main ingredient in chocolate is the bean of the cacao tree, which grows in the rain forests of South America.

Proteas

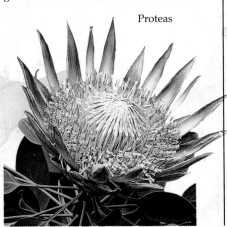

Fossils of the still-existing ginkgo tree (*Ginkgo biloba*) date back some 160 million years. It first appeared at the time of the dinosaurs, during the Jurassic period. Today, extract from the bark and root of the tree is considered to have medicinal benefits for humans. The seed kernel of the tree is a delicacy in China.

The raffia palm (*Raffia ruffia*) has the largest leaves of any plant, measuring up to more than 66 ft (20 m) in length.

The banyan tree (*Ficus benghalensis*) has aerial roots that grow down from the tree's branches and eventually form new trunks. In this way, the banyan grows both upward and downward.

Japan values the chrysanthemum flower highly. The country has dedicated a whole day (September 9) to the flower, and the *feng shui* tradition teaches that the chrysanthemum brings laughter and happiness to a home.

Tulips were originally native to Turkey, Iran, Syria, and parts of Asia before being brought to Europe by traveling merchants in the 16th century. The Dutch were the first European nation to cultivate tulips, doing so in 1593. By 1633, the Dutch upper classes were so gripped by "tulip mania" that individual bulbs were changing hands for huge sums of money.

The farthest known distance traveled by a drift seed is that of a plant called Mary's bean (*Merremia discoidesperma*), which traveled 15,000 miles (24,150 km) from the Marshall Islands to the coast of Norway.

Orchid

The color of the cherry is key to its survival

Q Why are the fruits of the cherry plant red?

A The fruits of the cherry plant are bright red in color to attract birds to eat the fruit as food. The cherries contain seeds that have a hard protective covering to ensure that when they are eaten by birds, the seeds will pass through the digestive system of the creatures unharmed. In this way, the seeds are safely spread, and the plant ensures its own survival. Plants pollinated by insects are rarely red because insects, with the exception of butterflies, cannot see red.

Q Which plant is considered to be the most bizarre of all?

A *Welwitschia mirabilis*, from the Namibian desert, is one of the strangest plants in the world. Known to live for up to 2,000 years, it has a stumpy stem and just two straplike leaves, which grow nonstop throughout its life. As the plant ages, its leaves become twisted and gnarled and can eventually be many yards long. The leaves are tough and woody—an adaptation that helps protect them from being eaten or drying out. *Welwitschia* survives in a region where there is little rain but where fog rolls in from the sea. The plant's leaves gather moisture from the fog, helping it survive. *Welwitschia* does not grow flowers but produces seeds in cones.

Q What is the richest plant region of the world?

A South America holds an estimated 90,000 species. Brazil leads the world as the country with the greatest known number of plant species, at 56,000, followed by Colombia, with 35,000. Mexico, Venezuela, Ecuador, Bolivia, and Peru are not far behind. The proliferation of plant species in this part of the world is thought to be due to the moist habitat associated with its tropical rain forests, as well as the relatively recent arrival of humans.

Q Why do some tree leaves change color in the fall?

A As the days become colder and shorter, chlorophyll, the green pigment in the leaves, breaks down and flows back into the tree. Meanwhile, waste products, such as tannins, pass out into the leaves. This chemical change produces browns and reds in the colors of the leaves as they die. Trees that lose their leaves are deciduous.

Record Breakers

Smallest plant
• The world's smallest flowering plant is duckweed, (*Wolffia angusta*). A tablespoon can hold more than 100,000 plants, and each measures only 0.031 in (0.8 mm) long and 0.016 in (0.4 mm) wide.

Largest seed
• The largest seed produced by any plant is that of the coco-de-mer (*Lodoicea maldivica*) from the Seychelles. This palm, also known as the double coconut tree, produces seeds that weigh up to 50 lb (23 kg) and take up to 10 years to grow into a tree.

Tallest tree
• The Mendocino coast redwood (*Sequoia sempervirens*), found in California, is the tallest tree in the world. The maximum height it has reached is 367.5 ft (112.01 m).

Duckweed

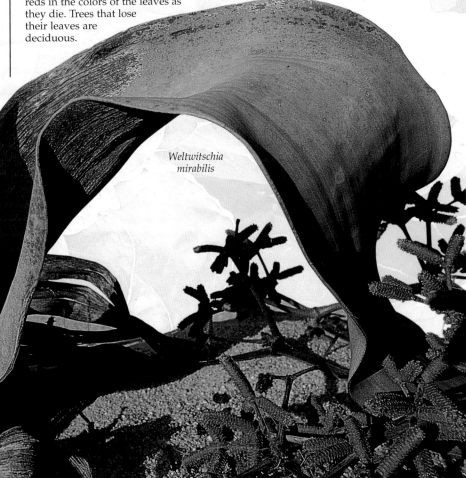

Weltwitschia mirabilis

Plant classification

Ginkgo

THE PLANT KINGDOM is divided into different groups and contains about 400,000 separate species that we know about. The majority of plant organisms belong to the flowering plant family called angiosperms. The groups shown here cover all of the main plant classifications.

Liverwort

Most liverworts have leaves but they can also be flat and leafless

GINKGO

The ginkgo, or maidenhair, tree is native to China. It is related to conifers but it has many unusual features, which is why it is classified in a group of its own. Unlike most conifers, ginkgos are deciduous, and they have fan-shaped leaves.

MOSSES AND LIVERWORTS

Mosses and liverworts belong to a group called the bryophytes, which number 14,000 species. These small plants usually grow in shaded, damp places. They first appeared around 425 million years ago and contributed to the formation of coal and peat.

FLOWERING PLANTS

Wheat

Flowering plants, or angiosperms, constitute about 300,000 species, the vast majority of plants. A flower is a specialized part of the plant and develops into a fruit, which contains one or more seeds housed in ovaries. These seeds must be pollinated and dispersed to ensure the continuation of each species. There are two types of flowering plants: monocots and dicots.

Rose

Monocots have a single cotyledon, or seedleaf. Their adult leaves are often long and narrow, with parallel veins. Monocots include cereals, such as wheat; some vegetables, such as leeks; some fruits, such as pineapples; and also orchids and lilies. They number about 55,000 species.

Dicots are plants whose seeds have two cotyledons, or seedleaves. Their adult leaves usually have a network of veins around a central midrib. Dicots total at least 250,000 species, and they include most shrubs and all the world's broadleaved trees.

Dicot plants often have woody stems.

Pineapple

Leek

Cabbage

Cactus

Clubmoss

CLUBMOSSES
Clubmosses, or lycopodophytes, existed as far back as 430 million years ago. Today's clubmosses are small, with overlapping leaves and creeping stems, but some prehistoric clubmosses grew into giant trees. Clubmosses reproduce by growing spores.

FERNS
Also known as pteridophytes, ferns include around 12,000 species and thrive in damp environments, such as forests. Fern leaves are called fronds and carry spores on the underside. These spores produce tiny plants that reproduce in turn, giving rise to the next generation of adult ferns.

CONIFERS
This group of about 550 species is mostly comprised of large evergreen trees. Conifers can photosynthesize even in winter and are often characterized by needle-shaped leaves. This group includes pines, firs, spruces, cedars, cypresses, and yews.

Pine

CYCADS
Cycads, which are gymnosperms, grow in the tropics. Although similar in appearance, they are not related to palms. Abundant in the Jurassic period, there are now just 100 species left. Their attractive leaves make them popular garden plants.

Cycad

HORSETAILS
These ancient plants are called sphenophytes. Around 300 million years ago they reached heights of 49 ft (15 m). Today there are only about 35 species left. This family is closely related to the fern group.

Vast horsetail forests once grew on Earth.

Horsetail

Weltwitschia mirabilis, also known as the tumboa

GNETOPHYTES
Cone-bearing desert plants, or gnetophytes, resemble flowering plants in many ways and were once thought to be a missing link between conifers and angiosperms. There are about 70 species in existence today.

Cones are produced during the summer months.

Find out more

IF YOU WOULD LIKE TO find out more about plants, you won't have to search far. Indeed, you only have to look around you. Go exploring in your own garden or start a window box. Armed with a plant identification handbook, take a walk in your local park or nature preserve, where you will find plenty of specimens to admire and study. For more exotic species and a wealth of information, visit a botanical garden. To check out ancient plant fossils, take a trip to a natural history museum. Flower markets can also be an interesting and colorful experience.

If an area of land is privately owned, always seek permission from the owner before exploring.

GO WILD
To see plants in a completely natural setting, just head for your local nature preserve (bring an adult with you). Spring is a good time to observe budding flowers and new shoots. Few sights compare to the vivid beauty of a meadow in midsummer bloom with wildflowers.

Wildflowers should not be picked, as this would disturb the natural environment

This garden pansy will lose some of its color as it dries.

BOTANICAL GARDENS
A botanical garden is dedicated to plants from around the world. Rare and exotic species are cultivated, often in specially controlled environments such as greenhouses. Desert plants, for example, must be kept in a hot, dry climate for survival.

When the flower is dry, write the plant name and date picked on the sheet of paper.

COLLECTING DRIED FLOWERS
Pick a flower in full bloom. Detach the flower head and leaves and place them flat on a sheet of blotting paper. Fold and enclose the sheet between the pages of a heavy book and allow to dry for a few weeks.

Places to Visit

MISSOURI BOTANICAL GARDEN, ST. LOUIS, MISSOURI
Features a variety of themed gardens, including the largest Japanese garden in North America, plus the Climatron, the world's first geodesic dome greenhouse.

NEW ORLEANS BOTANICAL GARDEN, NEW ORLEANS, LOUISIANA
An Art Deco botanical garden focusing on the plants of the Gulf South.

DESERT BOTANICAL GARDEN, PHOENIX, ARIZONA
Plants of the desert are the centerpiece here. Visit Plants and People of the Sonoran Trail, where visitors can twist agave fibers into twine, and four other trails.

NEW YORK BOTANICAL GARDEN, BRONX, NEW YORK
Features a Victorian-era greenhouse, the Enid A. Haupt Conservatory, and a children's garden.

WOODLAND WALKS
There are many official nature walks that choose specific routes best suited to the time of year. The organized walk below follows a path that takes ramblers through the first colorful crop of springtime bluebells.

ORNAMENTAL BUNCHES
A bouquet of flowers doesn't have to fade away. Its beauty can be preserved by taking it out of water and keeping it in a safe place until each stem has dried. Tie with a ribbon and place in a vase or on the wall.

This bunch of flowers was purchased at a flower market.

IN YOUR OWN BACK YARD
If you have a yard, this is the best place to find out more about plants. Using a notebook, you can log the growth and development of various species through the seasons. You can also grow your own plants.

ROOM WITH A VIEW
If you don't have access to a yard, window boxes make very rewarding miniature gardens. Flowers and herbs can be grown in any container and placed on a window ledge. Another way to grow plants outside is to cut an opening in a large bag of compost and use it as a soil bed.

Sunflower seeds should ideally be planted in May.

USEFUL WEB SITES

- All about gardening for kids, with great links:
  www.kidsgardening.com
- What can you do to help trees in the city? Visit this site for ideas:
  www.treesaremyfriends.org
- Funky gardening tips for beginners:
  www.yougrowgirl.com
- Missouri Botanical Gardens online:
  mbgnet.mobot.org
- Science projects and fun facts about botany:
  www.nbii.gov/disciplines/botany/science.html

Glossary

ACHENE A dry, one-seeded fruit. Plants in the buttercup family all have achenes.

ALGA A simple nonflowering plant that usually lives in water. Algae include seaweeds and many microscopic species.

ANGIOSPERM A flowering plant. Unlike gymnosperms, angiosperms grow their seeds inside a protective case called an ovary, which develops to form a fruit.

ANNUAL A plant that completes its life cycle within the growing season of one year

ANTHER The tip of a flower's stamen containing pollen

AXIL The angle between the upper part of a stem and a leaf or branch. Buds develop in the axil.

AXIS The main stem or root in a plant

BIENNIAL A plant that has two growing seasons. The seed is sown in the first year and flowers and fruits in its second year. The plant then dies.

BOTANY The scientific study of plants

BRACT A small leaflike flap that grows just beneath a flower

BUD The first visible sign of a new limb of a plant, or the protective case that encloses a flower that is still growing inside

Green alga, or seaweed

BULB An underground stem that stores food inside layers of fleshy scales. Plants use bulbs to survive drought or cold.

Stem and leaves sprouting from bulb

BULBIL A small bud that grows into an independent plant

BURR The prickly seedcase of some plants

CALYX The ring of sepals that protects a flower bud. The calyx often falls off when the flower blooms.

CARPEL The female organ of a flower, consisting of the stigma, the style, and the ovary

Daffodil bulbs

CELL The smallest possible unit of living matter, visible only under a microscope and consisting of a nucleus surrounded by cytoplasm and bound by a cell wall

CHLOROPHYLL The green pigment present in all plants and algae and involved in the process of photosynthesis

CHLOROPLAST A microscopic green structure, containing chlorophyll, that captures energy from sunlight inside plant cells

CLIMBER A plant that grows upward and outward, attaching itself to structures such as walls and fences

COROLLA The ring of petals in a flower

COTYLEDON A specialized leaf that is prepacked inside a seed. Cotyledons often look quite different from ordinary leaves.

DECIDUOUS A plant that loses its leaves seasonally

DICOT A plant whose seeds have two cotyledons. A dicot's leaves are often broad and have veins arranged in a network.

EMBRYO A young plant in its earliest stages of development

ENDOSPERM A supply of food that is stored inside a seed. The endosperm fuels the seedling's early growth.

EVERGREEN A plant that keeps its leaves year round, such as pines and firs

FILAMENT The stalk of a stamen, which supports the anther

FLORET A small flower that forms part of a composite flower, or flowerhead

GERMINATION When a seed begins to sprout and grow

GYMNOSPERM A plant whose seeds do not develop inside an ovary. Most gymnosperms are coniferous trees.

HARDY A plant that can withstand extremes of temperature, such as cold and frost

MONOCOT One of the two divisions of angiosperms. Monocots, or monocotyledons, are plants whose leaves have parallel veins. The other division of angiosperms is dicots.

MULTICELLULAR Comprised of more than one cell

A microscopic view of typical plant cells

NECTAR Naturally occurring sweet liquid found in the glands of many flowers

OVARY A female reproductive organ, which encloses fertilized seeds

OVULE A collection of female cells that form a seed after they have been fertilized by pollen

PAPPUS A ring or parachute of very fine hair that grows above a seed and helps it to be dispersed by the wind

PARACHUTE Any structure that aids the spread of seeds by the wind, such as a pappus

PARASITE An organism that lives in or on another organism, or host, from which it takes food and energy without giving anything back in return

PERENNIAL A plant that lasts or flowers for more than two years

PERIANTH The part of a flower made up of the calyx and the corolla together

PETAL A leafy flap in a flower, often brightly colored to attract animal pollinators

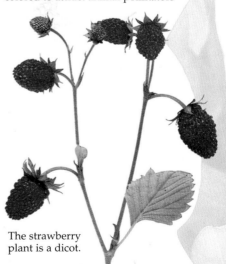

The strawberry plant is a dicot.

The bamboo plant is a monocot.

PHLOEM A system of cells that carries nutrients throughout a plant

PHOTOSYNTHESIS The process by which plants generate their own food, occurring when a green pigment called chlorophyll reacts with sunlight, carbon dioxide, and water to make carbohydrates, water, and oxygen

PIGMENT A colored chemical used by plants to collect light. One pigment, chlorophyll, makes plants look green.

PLANTLET A young plant, sometimes attached to its parent

PLUMULE The embryo shoot in a seed

POLLEN Microscopic grains containing male sex cells. Pollen is produced by the anthers of flowers.

POLLINATION The process by which pollen is carried from one flower to another. The male pollen fertilizes the female ovule and creates a seed. Insects and animals often carry pollen between flowering plants, or it can be blown by the wind.

RECEPTACLE The part of a plant that contains the flower, or, in flowerless plants, the reproductive organs or spores

RHIZOME A creeping underground stem. Rhizomes often sprout leaves as they push their way through the ground.

ROOT The part of a plant that anchors it to a solid surface, such as soil, and absorbs water and nutrients

RUNNER A stem that produces new plants by growing across the ground and sprouting roots

SEED A tough structure used by plants to reproduce. A seed contains a young plant, or embryo, together with all the food reserves it needs to start life on its own.

Poppy seeds carried on the wind

SEPAL A leafy flap that protects a flower while it is still a bud. Sepals often fall off when the flower opens.

SHOOT The parts of a plant above ground, including its stems, leaves, and flowers

SPADIX A fleshy spike of flowers

SPATHE A leaflike food that partly encloses a flowerhead

SPECIES A group of plants or other living things that look similar and that normally breed together in the wild

SPORE A single-celled reproductive unit of some organisms

SPUR A flowering or fruit-bearing branch that shoots out from an existing plant

STAMEN The pollen-producing part of a flower, consisting of a filament and an anther

STARCH The main food type stored in a plant. Chemically known as a carbohydrate, this food contains vital energy reserves.

STEM The part of a plant that carries the leaves. Also known as a stalk, the stem transports water and food from the roots to the rest of the plant.

STOMA An opening through which gases enter and leave the green part of a plant

TENDRIL A threadlike part of a plant that grows outward and wraps around nearby objects, helping the plant stay upright

TAPROOT A main root growing down

TEPAL A flap around a flower that works like a combination of a sepal and a petal

TENDER A plant that is sensitive to the cold

TESTA A hard shell of coating around a seed

TRANSPIRATION The movement of water through a plant. Water is taken up by the roots, and evaporates through pores in the leaves.

A variegated ivy leaf

TUBER A swelling or lump that forms in a root or stem and usually contains valuable food reserves for the rest of the plant. A potato is a tuber.

UMBEL An umbrella-shaped flowerhead

WHORL A collection of leaves, sepals, or petals growing in a circle around a plant stem

VARIEGATION Streaky or mottled, with contrasting colors. In plants, variegated leaves are caused by differences in the pigments across the leaf.

VEGETATION The plants found in a particular habitat or environment

XYLEM A system of cells that carries water through a plant. In shrubs and trees, toughened xylem cells form wood.

ZYGOTE A fertilized egg

Index

A

acacia, 36
achenes, 27
agrimony, 28
algae, 6, 7, 46
Allium paradoxum, 33
Aloe vera, 58
alpine plants, 50–51
annual, 13
ants, 36
anthers, 9, 12, 17, 18, 19, 20, 22, 23, 25
asparagus, 34
atropine, 59

B

bean, Mary's, 64
bear's-breeches, 20
bee pollination, 18, 19, 22, 23, 24, 26
belladonna, 59
biennial, 13
birds, 24, 26, 27
bladderworts, 40
blanketweed, 7
bracts, 25, 30, 31, 37
bread, 57
bromeliads, 46
buds, 9, 13, 14, 17, 38; flower, 9, 12, 16, 18, 26
bulbs, 11, 12, 33
bulbils, 33
bulrushes, 48
burrs, 28
butterfly pollination, 22, 23
butterworts, 40

C

cabbages, 55
cacti, 36, 52–53, 59
carnivorous plants, 40–41
carpel, 16, 17
carrot, 13, 21, 55
castor-oil plant, 58
chamomile, 21
chandelier plant, 32
chemicals, 36
cherry, 65
chicory, 54
chlorophyll, 14, 15, 65
chloroplasts, 15
chrysanthemum, 64
cinchona, 59
cladodes, 34
clematis, 21
climbers, 38–39
clubmosses, 6, 67
coal, 6
cobra lily, 41
coca, 59
cocaine, 59
coco-de-mer, 65
codeine, 58
coleoptile, 11
columbine, 29
conifers, 6, 7, 67
corm, 11
corn, 54
cotyledons, 10
creepers, 38–39, 46
creeping crowfoot, 32
crops, 54–55
cuckoopint, 11
cycads, 67

D

dandelion, 30–31
deadly nightshade, 59
deciduous, 37
defense, 36–37
diatoms, 7
dicotyledon, 8, 66
dodder, 44
dog rose, 20
drugs, 58, 59
duckweed, 65
durum wheat, 57

E F

eel-grass, 48
einkorn, 56
embryo, 10, 26
emmer, 56, 57
endosperm, 10, 26
enzymes, 43
ephemerals, 53
epiphytes, 38, 46, 47
eryngo, 21
eucalyptus, 34
evergreens, 35
fanwort, 48
ferns, 6, 67
fertilization, 11, 22, 26
filament, 17
florets, 21, 30; disc, 21
flowers, 6, 7, 12–13, 16–21, 22, 23, 24, 25, 26, 27, 30, 31, 48, 49, 50
fly pollination, 23, 24
foxglove, 59
fruit, 7, 13, 26–27, 28, 30, 31
fungus, 6

G H

germination, 10, 11
ginkgo, 64, 66
ginseng, 58
gnetophytes, 67
gourd, 38
gunneras, 34
gymnosperms, 6
Hart's-tongue fern, 6
haustoria, 44, 45
hemiparasite, 44
herb Robert, 34
heroin, 58
hibiscus, 25
Himalayan balsam, 18, 19, 29
hogweed, 21
holly, 37
honey guides, 12, 22
honeysuckle, 20
Hooker, William and Joseph, 60
horsetails, 6, 67
host plants, 44
hummingbirds, 25
hydrozoan, 6

I J K

insects, 12, 13, 16, 17, 18, 22-23, 24, 25, 30, 31, 36, 37, 40, 41, 42, 44
internode, 9
iris, 20, 33
ivy, 39
Jerusalem artichoke, 33
jojoba, 58
Josephine, Empress, 61
Joseph's coat, 35
kalanchoes, 32

L

leaf veins, 9, 32
leaves, 8, 10, 14, 15, 34–35, 40, 41, 42, 43, 46, 48, 49, 52, 53, 55
lesser burdock, 28
lianas, 46, 47
lichen, 6, 46
lily, 16, 17, 25, 34; water, 48, 49
liverworts, 6, 7
lotus, 28
lungwort, 35
lupine, 64

M N

malaria, 59
Malmaison, 43, 61
mandrake, 58
marjoram, 23
meadown cranesbill, 29
medicines, 58–59
mescal, 59
mescal cactus, 59
minerals, 8, 9
mistletoe, 44
monocotyledon, 9, 66
mosses, 6, 7, 46, 64, 66
mountain plants, 50–51
mullein, 20
nasturtium, 12–13
nectar, 12, 13, 18, 19, 22, 23, 24, 25, 41, 42
nettle, 36

O P

oil, 13, 15, 58
onion, 15, 33
opium, 58
orchids, 23, 24, 46, 47, 64; fly, 23; moth, 46, 47
ovary, 7, 13, 17, 26, 27
ovules, 13, 23, 26, 27
paddyfields, 55
palm, raffia, 64
pansy, 7
paper, 49
papyrus, 49
parasitic plants, 44–45
passion flower, 18
pasta, 57
perennial, 13, 33
perianth segments, 16, 17
petal, 9, 12, 13, 16, 17, 18, 19, 20, 21, 22, 24, 26, 27
phloem, 8, 9
phlox, 51
photosynthesis, 10, 14–15, 42
piggyback plant, 32
pine, Bristlecone, 64
pineapple, 46
pitcher plants, 40–41
plumule, 10
poisons, 58–59
pollen, 8, 9, 12, 17, 18, 22, 23, 25, 26, 27
pollination, 11, 17, 22–23, 24–25
polyps, 6
poppy, 13, 29, 58
potatoes, 14–15, 33, 54
prickly pear cactus, 52
proboscis, 24
pseudobulbs, 47
pumpkin, 64
pyrethrum, 34

Q R

quinine, 59
radicle, 10, 11
rafflesia, 20, 44–45
receptacle, 26, 27
redwood, 65
respiration, 8
rhizomes, 33
rhododendron, 35, 60
rice, 55
ricin, 58
rock roses, 51
root cap, 8
root hairs, 8, 10, 11, 15
rootless duckweed, 7
rootlets, 8
roots, 10, 13, 14, 15, 38, 39, 46, 47, 52, 53, 55
rose, 26–27, 37
rosebay willowherb, 20
rose hips, 26-27
runner bean, 10, 38, 39
runners, 32, 33

S

saguaro, 53
screw pine, 36
seed case, 10, 11, 29
seed dispersal, 26, 27, 28–29, 30–31
seed leaves, 10
seedling, 10, 28
seeds, 8, 10, 11, 13, 16, 19, 26, 27, 28, 29, 30, 31, 47, 50, 54, 56, 62
sepals, 9, 12, 13, 16, 17, 18, 19, 20, 26, 44
shoots, 8, 9, 14
silica, 7, 36
silversword, 50
spadix, 25
spearwort, 48
spelt wheat, 57
spines, 36, 37, 52

spirogyra, 7
spores, 6, 7
spurge, 52
stamens, 16, 17, 26, 27
starch, 14, 15
stigma, 9, 12, 16, 17, 18, 19, 20, 22, 23, 26
stings, 36
stolons, 32, 33
stomata, 52
strawberry plant, 32
style, 17, 18, 23, 26
succulents, 32, 52–53
suckers, 8, 39, 44
sugars, 8, 9, 15
sundews, 40, 41, 43
sunflower, 10, 21, 30
sweet pea, 20
Swiss cheese plant, 35
sycamore, 61

T U

teasel, 37
tendrils, 38-39
tepals, 16, 17, 21
testa, 10, 26
thallus, 7
thistle, 29, 30, 37
thorns, 36, 37
toadflax, 22, 29
tomato, 55
tradescantia, 61
Tradescant, John, 61
transpiration, 53
tree mallow, 9
tuber, 11, 14, 33
tulip, 20, 33, 60, 64
tumbleweed, 32
umbel, 21
umbellifers, 21
urn plant, 24

V W X

vegetative reproduction, 32–33
Venus flytrap, 40, 42–43
vetches, 29
water buttercup, 34
water lilies, 48, 49
water plants, 34, 48–49
waterwheel plant, 43
wellingtonias, 6, 7
Weltwitschia mirabilis, 65, 67
wheat, 56–57
wood cranesbill, 17
xylem, 8, 9

Acknowledgments

The publisher would like to thank:
Brinsley Burbidge, Valerie Whalley, John Lonsdale, Milan Swaderlig, Andrew McRobb, Marilyn Ward, and Pat Griggs of the Royal Botanic Gardens, Kew, England. Arthur Chater at the Natural History Museum.
David Burnie for consultancy.
Dave King for special photography on pages 8–9.
Fred Ford and Mike Pilley at Radius for artwork.

Picture credits
t=top, b=bottom, m=middle, l=left, r=right
A-Z Botanical: 55m
Heather Angel/Biofotos: 43tm; 49ml
V. Angel/Daily Telegraph Colour Library: 39bm
Australian High Commission: 24tr; 57tr
A.N.T./NHPA: 25mr
J. and M. Bain/NHPA: 11bl
G.I. Bernard/Oxford Scientific Films: 7tl; 46br
G.I. Bernard/NHPA: 15tr; 18mr; 36m; 40mr
Deni Bown/Oxford Scientific Films: 64bc
Bridgeman Art Library: 55mb; 58br
Brinsley Burbidge/Royal Botanic Gardens, Kew: 50bm; 58m
M.Z. Capell/ZEFA: 10tr
James H. Carmichael/NHPA: 53br
Gene Cox/Science Photo Library: 7m
Stephen Dalton/NHPA: 19tr; 22ml; 30tl; 36tr; 40ml
P. Dayanandan/Science Photo Library: 9tl

Jack Dermid/Oxford Scientific Films: 32br
Dr. Dransfield/Royal Botanic Gardens, Kew 45
Mary Evans Picture Library: 44 tl; 46bl; 48ml; 56tl, tr; 60tr; 61br; 62tm
Patrick Fagot/NHPA: 71bl
Robert Francis/South American Pictures: 54tl
Linda Gamlin: 27mr; 29bm
Brian Hawkes/NHPA: 23tl
Hulton Picture Library: 42tl
E.A. Janes/NHPA: 28bl; 68br
Peter Lillie/Oxford Scientific Films: 65b; 67b
Patrick Lynch/Science Photo Library: 6tm; 8br
Mansell Collection: 8bl; 59bm
Marion Morrison/South American Pictures: 59m
Peter Newark's Western Americana: 52br
Oxford Scientific Films: 66tl

Brian M. Rogers/Biofotos: 46bm
Royal Botanic Gardens, Kew: 16tl; 43tl; 60m; 61m
John Shaw/NHPA: 9tr; 64tl, br
Survival Anglia: 7tl
Silvestris Fotoservice/FLPA: 65tl
John Walsh/Science Photo Library: 15tl
M.I. Walker/NHPA: 70tr
J. Watkins/Frank Lane Picture Agency: 50bl
Alan Williams: 68tr
Rogers Wilmshurst/Frank Lane: 26tr
David Woodfall/NHPA: 68c
Steven Wooster: 69tr
Jacket images: Front: Bill Ross/Corbis, b; Peter Lillie/OSF, tl; Mary Evans Picture Library, tcr.
Illustrations by: Sandra Pond and Will Giles: 12–13, 17, 38
Picture research by: Angela Jones and Lorna Ainger